The Stressed out Dentist's Guide to Dental Law

What your regulators won't tell you and what the lawyers don't want you to know.

First publication in Great Britain

By SNH Publications Ltd

Visit the author's website at www.gdpresources.com

Acknowledgement is made for permission to quote copyrighted materials

Printed in Great Britain

Contents

Disclaimer & NOTICE

For legal reasons, I am obliged to state the following:

To the fullest extent permitted by law, SNH Publications Ltd are providing this written material, its subsidiary elements and its contents on an "as is" basis and make no (and expressly disclaim all) representations or warranties of any kind with respect to this material or its contents including, without limitation, advice and recommendations, warranties or merchantability and fitness for a particular purpose. The author is NOT a lawyer and is giving his interpretation of dental law based on the information available to him in the public domain. This should therefore not be seen as giving legal advice.

If you face any kind of legal challenge in your dental practice, PLEASE CONSULT YOUR INDEMNIFIER

The information is given for entertainment purposes only.

In addition, SNH Publications Ltd do not represent or warrant that the information accessible via this material is accurate, complete or current because the law changes frequently. To the fullest extent permitted by law, neither SNH Publications Ltd nor any of its affiliates, partners, directors, employees or other representatives will be liable for damages arising out of or in connection with the use of this material. This is a comprehensive limitation of liability that applies to all damages of any kind, including (without limitation) compensatory, direct, indirect or consequential damages, loss of data, income or profit, loss or damage to property and claims of third parties. Any dispute will be under the jurisdiction of the English Courts.

Acknowledgment

I would like to thank the following people who helped with the proof reading:

- Matthew Pring

- Ian Jones

- Susan Hudson

Thank you for buying this book. Because of your trust I would like to give you a free gift. If you sign up to my free newsletter at **www.gdpresources.co.uk** and you will receive an email with a download link to a RESTORATIVE RECORD KEEPING TEMPLATE. Put together by several top restorative dentists, it shows what we feel you should be recording in the dental notes for your protection.

Introduction

This is an exciting time to be alive as a Dentist. Technology and our understanding of the process of dental disease is making it easier to treat and prevent that disease. We can do more with less and restore dentitions that have been decimated by decay and old style dentistry. Unfortunately, there are also challenges. Patient expectations can be high, and the demands for an acceptable "customer service experience" is ever present. But more importantly to us, the rise of regulatory complaints, litigation and the interference into our affairs by external agencies is becoming an ever growing burden.

We cannot continue to do what we used to do. The present environment now demands we change and adapt. To do otherwise will see us swept away as a profession. The days when we could just put a dental chair in a room and treat patients are long since passed. The days when you could write Exam S/P in the notes are now akin to myth and legend.

We have to be the ones to adapt because the environment we work in isn't going to change any time soon. Politicians do not care about dentists, that is a fact. And there are some who would say we are nothing more than an irritant to a parliament that arguably wants to remove dentistry from the NHS altogether. I can't comment on that. What I can say is that despite the burdens placed upon us, there is still the opportunity to grow and thrive as dentists.

Just remember that the rules have changed. And in a way, they have changed for the better, despite the doom and gloom. Gone are the practices with dubious cross infection control procedures. No longer can a dentist Lord over his staff and his patients with impunity. We are entering into the age of equality where the professions complimentary to dentists attain the respect they rightfully deserve.

You show me an astounding dentist, and I will show you the Nursing and Reception team that help make him/her so. It's a team effort, just as it always has been. Only now we are starting to accept that and admit it. But if the rules have changed, we need to know what the new rules are. We need to understand the legal and regulatory framework we now work under. We can no longer be ignorant of our responsibilities despite any reservations we may have. This book is one man's attempt to put it all together in one place. But you need to understand that the law is constantly changing. By the time you get to read this book, dear reader, parts of it may have become obsolete. So here is the most important statement I will make in the entire book. Ignore it at your peril.

If at any time you have a concern to do with any legal aspect of your existence as a dentist, **contact your indemnifier and ASK THEM**. That is what they are there for. That is what you pay them for. Whilst I will do everything in my ability to get the information I put in this book right, please remember that I am not a lawyer. I'm just a bloke trying to help (if you haven't already done so, please read the disclaimer). This book is a starting point and is no replacement for proper legal advice. My hope though, is that it will make you think.

So how do we begin? Well, when you graduated, some of you may remember reciting the Hippocratic oath, a tearful moment for many a weeping mother in the audience (not all universities get graduates to recite this oath). For those who did, do you remember it? Here is a reminder of the full modern text which might differ from what you spoke that fateful day:

"- I swear to fulfil, to the best of my ability and judgment, this covenant:
- I will respect the hard-won scientific gains of those physicians in whose steps I walk, and gladly share such knowledge as is mine with those who are to follow.
- I will apply, for the benefit of the sick, all measures [that] are required, avoiding those twin traps of overtreatment and therapeutic nihilism.
- I will remember that there is art to medicine as well as science, and that warmth, sympathy, and understanding may outweigh the surgeon's knife or the chemist's drug.
- I will not be ashamed to say "I know not," nor will I fail to call in my colleagues when the skills of another are needed for a patient's recovery.
- I will respect the privacy of my patients, for their problems are not disclosed to me that the world may know. Most especially must
- I tread with care in matters of life and death. If it is given me to save a life, all thanks. But it may also be within my power to take a life; this awesome responsibility must be faced with great humbleness and awareness of my own frailty. Above all, I must not play at God.
- I will remember that I do not treat a fever chart, a cancerous growth, but a sick human being, whose illness may affect the person's family and economic stability. My responsibility includes these related problems, if I am to care adequately for the sick.
- I will prevent disease whenever I can, for prevention is preferable to cure.
- I will remember that I remain a member of society, with special obligations to all my fellow human beings, those sound of mind and body as well as the infirm.
- If I do not violate this oath, may I enjoy life and art, respected while I live and remembered with affection thereafter. May I always act so as to preserve the finest traditions of my calling

and may I long experience the joy of healing those seeking my help."

Perhaps a more up to date version is the Declaration of Geneva, published by the World Medical Association:

- I solemnly pledge to consecrate my life to the service of humanity;
- I will give to my teachers the respect and gratitude that is their due;
- I will practise my profession with conscience and dignity;
- The health of my patient will be my first consideration;
- I will respect the secrets that are confided in me, even after the patient has died;
- I will maintain by all the means in my power, the honour and the noble traditions of the medical profession;
- My colleagues will be my sisters and brothers;
- I will not permit considerations of age, disease or disability, creed, ethnic origin, gender, nationality, political affiliation, race, sexual orientation, social standing or any other factor to intervene between my duty and my patient;
- I will maintain the utmost respect for human life;
- I will not use my medical knowledge to violate human rights and civil liberties, even under threat;
- I make these promises solemnly, freely and upon my honour

One final thing to note. This book is not just supposed to be a reference manual. I also envisage it being a learning tool.

Regulation

You, as a dentist effectively have two regulators. The General Dental Council (GDC) and the Care Quality Commission (CQC). If you work in the NHS or under NHS contract, the Department of Health will also carry a regulatory duty over you in some aspects.

The GDC

The GDC are given its powers by the **Dentist Act (1984)**[1]**.** This act gives the GDC specific responsibilities in its regulation of dentistry:

- To protect the public
- To protect, promote and maintain the health, safety and well-being of the public
- To promote and maintain confidence in the dental profession
- To promote and maintain proper professional standards and conduct for members of those professions
- To grant registration only to those dental professionals who meet the requirements on education and training, health and good character. Only those who are registered with the GDC can practice dentistry in the UK
- To set standards for providers of dental education and training in the UK. To set standards of conduct, performance and ethics for the dental team
- To investigate complaints against dental professionals and where appropriate take action through our fitness to practise process

- To require dental professionals to keep their skills up to date through continuing professional development requirements.
- Collects the fee that allows a dental registrant to remain on the register that the GDC maintains
- Prosecute illegal practice
- Sets the standards for oversees dentists working in UK

All paid for by your ARF. Doesn't that just give you a warm glow inside? This however is the essence of self-regulation, and you as a registrant are only able to work as a dentist because of your registration with the General Dental Council. This is why talk of withholding ones ARF in protest of recent GDC decisions are fraught with difficulty. The GDC are the sole arbiter of who can and cannot practice dentistry, powers given to them by statute law. If you don't pay your ARF you are no longer legally allowed to treat your patients and open yourself up to criminal and regulatory proceedings.

Just as someone who drives a car is not expected to have read the **Road Traffic Act**, so you as a Dentist are not to be expected to have read the **Dentist Act 1984**, although this author recommends that you do so. However, as a car driver you are expected to be familiar with the laws and regulations that govern your conduct on the roads, as set out in the Highway Code. The GDC have their version of this in their document, **Standards for the Dental Team**. It is essential you have read and understood these standards, and a useful guide to this can be found at the following GDC website at:

https://standards.gdc-uk.org/[2]

However, there are additional documents to consider other than the standards:

- **Guidance on advertising**
- **Guidance on child protection and vulnerable adults**
- **Guidance on commissioning/ manufacturing appliances**
- **Guidance on indemnity**
- **Guidance on prescribing medicines**
- **Guidance on reporting criminal proceedings**
- **Guidance on using social media**

All can be found on the GDC website at:

https://www.gdc-uk.org/professionals/standards/team[3]

The GDC has undergone several changes over the last fifteen years, in part due to the Shipman outrage. Registrants are now more likely to experience an investigation by the GDC than even say ten years ago. The reasons for this are varied, but some of them may include:

- A greater willingness for patients to complain about their dental care and a greater willingness of some in the profession to recommend patients seek redress for past care via the GDC
- A reported pattern of referral to the GDC by Local Area Teams as a means to deal with patient complaints about NHS care
- Advertising by the GDC to increase awareness amongst the public
- An NHS system that has introduced vagueness and uncertainty about what can and cannot be done under NHS contract.
- Reports of some law firms encouraging their clients to complain to the GDC, although I have yet to see proof of this.

- A downgrading in the burden of proof necessary from the criminal to the civil standard
- A reinforcement of what the CQC refer to as the "duty of candour" which makes it an obligation for professionals to report breaches in the standards by other professionals

On that last point, the GDC now require every registered dental professional to raise concerns where they feel patients or fellow professionals are at risk. This will be discussed later on in this book.

The GDC can receive complaints from a variety of sources. Patients, Local Area teams, other dental professionals, the police and members of the public can all raise concerns about a registrant's fitness to practice. A registrant's health, performance and conduct can all result in a fitness to practice referral. It is important for you to remember that the GDC MUST investigate all allegations that are put to them. They have no choice in the matter. However recent changes show more emphasis on local resolution. So if for example a complaint is received about NHS care, there is now an increased likelihood that the complainant will be referred to the LAT team which run the particular dentist's contract.

Fitness to Practice

The fitness to practice rules that the GDC work to are actually set out in a statutory instrument called **"The General Dental Council (Fitness to Practise) Rules Order of Council 2006"**[4] When investigating registrants, the GDC is given powers handed down by parliament to determine whether a dentist has fallen short of the expected standards.

- The fitness to practise process of the GDC comes from its duty to maintain the integrity of the dental register. Regulating professionals and dealing with underperformance and severe misconduct is essential for the GDC to meet the requirements set out in the Dentist Act 1984.
- The GDC outlines how it expects registrants to behave in its guidance documents and in its standards. The standards are freely available in book format and online
- Failure to comply with the standards may lead to fitness to practice proceedings.
- For the GDC to impose severe sanctions or remove you from the register (either temporarily or permanently) they need to prove to the fitness to practice committee that your impairment fell far below the expected standard and that you are also currently impaired.
- The fitness to practice committee act as judge and jury, the defence and the prosecution both making their case with the help of expert witnesses (dentists who act to give their expert opinion on the matters at hand).
- Your impairment, or lack of, will be judged "on the balance of probability" which is the civil standard rather than "beyond reasonable doubt", which is the criminal standard.
- Complainants cannot be sued for defamation if they make a complaint to the regulator even if that complaint is malicious or vexatious. Although complainants do have to give their evidence under oath, they do not have to sign a statutory declaration that what they are saying is the truth (which was once a requirement).

Much of the fitness to practice process is based on the investigation of a professional's fitness to practice. A registrant's (that would be you dear reader) fitness to practice can be impaired (and remember the importance is whether it is currently impaired) by reason of:

- Misconduct
- Deficient professional performance
- Adverse physical or mental health
- A conviction or caution
- A decision by another regulatory body
- A lack of sufficient indemnity/insurance
- An accusation of dishonesty

Misconduct

A regulator should only become involved where the misconduct alleged is of a serious nature. It is however surprisingly difficult to find what the definition of "misconduct" actually is which some of you might find surprising considering the serious implications that such a charge implies. As a consequence, over the years various appeals courts have given their version of what they determine the phrase "professional misconduct" actually means. Unfortunately, without a defined definition there will always be borderline cases and differences of opinion. For example, several cases that went to full fitness to practice hearings in 2016 had the result of "no case to answer" which reflects this borderline issue and gives an indication of why changes were needed.

The General Medical Council define misconduct as a "Serious and Persistent failure to follow the guidance". This definition can be found in the GMC publication Good Medical practice[5].

In the legal case **Roylance v General Medical Council**[6] in 2000 the judge said:

"Misconduct is a word of general effect, involving some act or omission which falls short of what would be proper in the circumstances. The standard of propriety may often be found by reference to the rules and standards ordinarily required to be followed by a medical practitioner in the particular circumstances".

The GDC fortunately do have a definition of Misconduct based on existing case law (which means they didn't technically come up with the definition themselves). There are basically two types of misconduct, and I quote from the "GDC case examiner manual" with permission[7]:

1) It may involve sufficiently serious misconduct in the exercise of professional practice. In those circumstances:

i. *Misconduct denotes serious acts or omissions, suggesting a significant departure from what would be proper in the circumstances;*
ii. *In respect of clinical matters, mere negligence does not constitute misconduct. Nevertheless, and depending upon the circumstances, negligent acts or omissions which are particularly serious may amount to misconduct;*
iii. *A single negligent act or omission is less likely to cross the threshold of misconduct than multiple acts or omissions. Nevertheless, and depending upon the circumstances, a single negligent act or omission, if particularly grave, could be characterised as misconduct;*
iv. *Misconduct need not arise in the context of clinical practice, but must be in the exercise of a registrant's calling as a dental professional. Such misconduct may*

properly be described as linked to the practice of dentistry, even though it involves the exercise of administrative or managerial functions, where they are part of the day to day practice of a registrant, and where, depending on the nature of the duties, a continuing obligation to focus on patient care may exist; and

v. *Misconduct may also fall within the scope of a registrant's calling as a dental professional where there is no direct link with clinical practice at all – for example, acting as an expert witness, or being involved in education or research where the registrant's skills are directly engaged.*

2) Misconduct can involve conduct of a disreputable, morally culpable or otherwise disgraceful kind which may, and often will, occur outside the course of professional practice itself, but which brings disgrace upon the registrant and thereby prejudices the reputation of the profession (we are seeing a fair bit of such from the acting profession at present). In those circumstances:

i. *it does not matter whether such conduct is directly related to the exercise of professional skills; and*

ii. *action taken in good faith and for legitimate reasons, however inefficient or ill-judged, is not capable of constituting misconduct merely because it might damage the reputation of the profession.*

Misconduct can also include a failure to follow the guidance and standards as laid out by the GDC (remember though that apart from anything published by themselves, the GDC will rarely tell you the specific guidance or standards they expect you to follow). Quite a mouthful all that wouldn't you say?

Deficient professional performance

The GDC's definition of deficient professional performance is as follows

i. *A standard of professional performance which is unacceptably low and which (save in exceptional circumstances) has been demonstrated by reference to a fair sample of the registrant's work. A single instance of negligent treatment, unless very serious indeed, would be unlikely to constitute deficient professional performance;*

ii. *Poor judgment cannot in itself constitute gross negligence or negligence of a high degree, but it may in an appropriate case, and particularly if exercised over a period of time, constitute seriously deficient performance;*

iii. *deficient performance may in principle arise from the inadequate performance of any function which is part of a registrant's calling as a dental professional. Which charge is appropriate depends on the gravity of the alleged incompetence. Incompetence falling short of gross negligence but which is still seriously deficient will fall under deficient professional performance rather than misconduct.*

The Fitness to practise process

The GDC concentrates on your fitness to practise as a registrant. When a complaint is received by the GDC, it is examined by a caseworker to ensure it is within the GDC's remit. If it is, the case is passed onto the case examiners. We will now look at the process involved:

1) Case examiners

These work in pairs and consist of one registrant and one lay person. Case examiners are employees of the GDC, and unlike expert witnesses are not independent. They decide whether the case needs to go further to a public hearing (they need to be assured that there is a likelihood that the registrants current fitness to practise is impaired). The case examiners will make one of several decisions:

- **Take no further action**
- **Give the dental professional advice or a warning**
- **Set conditions on the registrant's registration**
- **Adjourn the case to seek further information**
- **Refer the matter to a practise committee including the Interim Orders Committee**

2) Practise committees

There are several practise committees, the members of which are independent and drawn from a pool of dental professionals and lay people. This is known as the Fitness to Practice Panel.

- **The Professional Conduct Committee** (PCC) is charged with determining whether or not a dental professional's fitness to practise is impaired on the basis of the facts found proved. Where a registrant's fitness to practise is found to be impaired the PCC decides whether to impose a sanction. The PCC can conclude that the registrant's fitness to practise is not impaired and close the case, issue a reprimand, impose conditions for up to 36 months (with a review - immediate conditions can be applied if required), suspend the registrant for up to 12 months (with or without a review. Immediate suspension can be applied if required) or erase the registrant from the Register.

- **The Professional Performance Committee** (PPC) deals with cases where it appears that a dental professional's performance is consistently falling below an acceptable standard. The PPC can conclude that the registrant's fitness to practise is not impaired and close the case, issue a reprimand, impose conditions for up to 36 months (with a review. Immediate conditions can be applied if required), suspend the registrant for up to 12 months (with or without a review. Immediate suspension can be applied if required) or erase the registrant from the Register.
- **The Health Committee** (HC) deals with cases where the dental professional's fitness to practise is impaired by reason of ill health. After consideration the Health Committee may: Conclude that the registrant's fitness to practise is not impaired and close the case, issue a reprimand, impose conditions for up to 36 months (with a review) or suspend the registrant for up to 12 months (with or without a review. Immediate suspension can be applied if required). The Health committee can also refer the case back to the lower tiers of the FTP pathway, as well as referring to one of the other committees.
- **The Interim Orders Committee** (IOC) can, as an interim measure, suspend or place conditions upon a dental professional before a full inquiry by a PC. The suspension may be renewed or revoked later. At this stage it is important to note that the allegations have not been tested or proved - this is the work of the other practice committees. A case can be referred to the IOC at any stage.

It is important to repeat the fact that the Interim Orders Committee can impose sanction BEFORE a public hearing has gone ahead.

They will only do this where they feel the safety of the public is an immediate issue with the registrant.

Once a practice committee is involved, this is where the lawyers and the expert witnesses enter the fray. Whilst the lawyers will do what they can for their side “to win” (I have yet to meet a lawyer or barrister who liked loosing) the expert witnesses have a duty to be impartial. There has been considerable concern over recent years about the impartiality of expert witnesses, with some notable cases where GDC expert witnesses were clearly biased in their evidence. It is not in the remit of the book to highlight individual cases, and you can be reassured that the GDC are taking measures to address this issue. Should a registrant be called before a committee however, it is imperative that they have decent and competent legal representation because that can make the difference between continuing to practice and being struck off.

At a full hearing both the prosecution (the GDC) and the defence will have an opportunity to present their case. Both sides will present evidence and call witnesses. If the expert witnesses for both sides have not been able to agree on the facts as they see them (and thus present a joint statement) both expert witnesses will be called to appear so that their evidence can be cross examined. It will then be for the panel to decide on the judgment based on their opinion of the evidence provided.

If your hearing goes against you, you can still appeal to the High Court. If the High Court finds in your favour, it will either send the case back to one of the committees, substitute the decision for one of its own or quash the decision altogether. Should you be called before them, the GDC will want to see that you are open, honest, able to reflect and have the ability to learn from any mistakes made. They also require you to show you have improved your practice in relation to what you have been accused of. Many a dentist has saved their career by making changes and showing that they were no longer currently impaired. Many a dentist has lost their career by taking a belligerent and defiant attitude.

A list of charges that have been historically levelled against registrants has been included in **Appendix 1.** A list of CPD requirements that the GDC mandates (at the time of writing) can be found in **Appendix 2.**

The Professional Standards Authority (PSA)

The PSA is the GDC's regulator. They report on the GDC's performance and offer advice and guidance. Unfortunately, they don't really have any "teeth" and also are there to make sure the GDC haven't been too lenient. They can appeal a practice committee decision if they feel that the outcome was not sufficient for the protection of the public. In other words, if they feel the "Independent practise committee" have been too soft on the registrant, the PCC can bring the matter back onto the table. I want you to imagine that for a second. You get through a hearing and save your registration, only for the letter to land on your doormat at a later date saying the case is being referred back to the GDC.

The Care Quality Commission (CQC)

The CQC is a non-departmental public body (NDPB) of the Department of Health (DOH). The CQC was brought into existence by the Health and Social Care Act 2008[8] and was an amalgamation of the **Healthcare Commission**, the **Commission**

for Social Care Inspection and the **Mental Health Act Commission**.

To provide dental care in England and Wales, the practice has to be registered with the CQC. The CQC are charged to set and maintain standards, and part of your registration with them will involve regular inspection to ensure you meet the standards set out by them. Due to what was found when inspections started, dental practices are felt to be low risk by the CQC. Whilst an inspection can be a routine affair with prior warning, they may inspect without warning if they receive information that you are in breach of their standards. It is beyond the scope of this book to examine how the CQC regulates dental practices. Instead we would refer you to the CQC's own guidance documents

- **How CQC Regulates: Primary care dental Services, Provider handbook. March 2015**[9]
- **CQC, The scope of registration - Registration under the Health and Social Care Act 2008**[10]

Part of your duty as a registered health care practice is to notify the CQC about certain changes, events and incidents that affect the service to people who use it. They have a specific page on their website specifically with regards to this[11]. The things you are required to notify the CQC regarding are (and further guidance can be obtained from the CQC website[12]):

- **Absence of a registered individual from the premises for more than 28 days** (so if you go on a long holiday….)
- **The return of said individual after 28 days**
- **Allegations of abuse** (safeguarding where people attending your practice are the victim/ perpetrator of the abuse, or both)
- **Changes to registered practice's details**
- **Changes to the name and/or details of the registered manager** (So if you get married and change your name or get more letters after your name is this notifiable perhaps?)

- **Notification of service provider's insolvency**
- **Changes to organisation's nominated individuals, officers and directors**
- **When partners join or leave a partnership**
- **If you plan to stop providing regulated activities**
- **If the provider changes their name or address**
- **When the registered manager for one or more of your registered activities changes**
- **If you change your statement of purpose**
- **Death of a person using the service or Death of a registered provider**
- **If anything stops you running the service safely and properly** (A flood or a break in might apply here. It even applies if the surgery can't open because of snow.)
- **Police involvement in an incident** (so you know when Mr Miggins was kicking off about his denture and you felt compelled to phone the police…)
- **Serious injury to a person using a service** (injury to staff comes under HSE RIDDOR)

That last one needs closer inspection, because what exactly is the definition of a serious injury? Well, helpfully there is no actual definition. The CQC do provide some examples however:

- **Permanent disfigurement, such as a burn or scarring**.
- **An injury that requires surgery to remedy** (root into the sinus for example).
- **Temporary, semi-permanent or permanent harm, for example, as a consequence of a drug error** (most likely would include lip numbness due to a lower 8 or ID block).
- **Injuries that damage any major organs of the body, for example, a perforation** (even where this may be a known complication of the procedure).
- **Injuries that cause loss of any senses such as blindness. Actual serious injury or harm to a patient, as a result**

of failure of establishment systems, procedures, guidelines or protocols, including breach of confidentiality.

Penalties

The penalties for not meeting CQC standards and reporting requirements can be severe. Whilst the GDC can stop you working, the CQC can shut down your whole surgery. The powers of the CQC are varied. They can

- **Issue notices to set out what improvements the care provider must take and by when**
- **Make changes to the care provider's registration to limit what they may do, for example by imposing conditions**
- **Place a provider in special measures where the CQC closely supervise the care provided whilst helping the provider to improve the care**
- **Issues cautions, fines, and even prosecute through the courts.**

A list of incidents where the CQC may prosecute breaches directly without first issuing a warning notice can be found here - **http://www.cqc.org.uk/guidance-providers/regulations-enforcement/offences**[13]

Just as with the GDC, I hope you can appreciate that the CQC are not an agency you want to mess about with. There is something interesting to note however. In 2013 the Robert Francis report was released in response to the utter insanity that occurred in the Mid Staffordshire NHS Foundation Trust between 2005-2009. The report was very critical of the regulators in general. The difference between the GDC and the CQC is that the CQC took on board the Francis report fully, and even employed

Lord Francis as an advisor. And although the inspections are now more thorough, they are also rarer and more intelligence led. They have accepted that dental practices are low risk, and the new regime allows them to concentrate on where the problem actually lies. So whilst you now only have a 10% chance of your practice being inspected in any one year, it is much more difficult to pass said inspection than when the CQC first arrived on the scene.

The NHS

The provision of NHS dentistry under the National Health Service Act 1977 is also regulated by the various statutory instrument:

- **The National Health Service (General Dental Services Contracts) Regulations 2005[14]**
- **The National Health Service (Personal Dental Services Agreements) Regulations 2005[15]**
- **The National Health Service (General Dental Services Contracts) (Wales) Regulations 2006[16]**
- **The National Health Service (Personal Dental Services Agreements) (Wales) Regulations 2006[17]**
- **The National Health Service (Dental Charges) Regulations 2005[28]**

There may well be more legislation hiding away somewhere (there was an update to the contract in 2013 for example). It is therefore important that you read your contract and the Dental Charges Regulations. The challenge here is that many of the provisions in these Statutory Instruments are vague and open to interpretation. This can result in dentists unwittingly falling foul by doing treatment that they believe is in the patient's best interests.

The 2006 contract does give representatives of the NHS the right to inspect your practice

Part 6, Schedule 3, Entry and inspection by the Primary Care Trust
44.—(1) Subject to—
(a) the conditions in sub-paragraph (2); and
(b) sub-paragraph (3), the contractor shall allow persons authorised in writing by the Primary Care Trust to enter and inspect the practice premises at any reasonable time.
(2) The conditions referred to in sub-paragraph (1) are that—
(a) reasonable notice of the intended entry has been given;
(b) written evidence of the authority of the person seeking entry is produced to the contractor on request; and
(c) entry is not made to any premises or part of the premises used as residential accommodation without the consent of the resident.

National Institute for health and Care Excellence (NICE)[19]

GDP's providing care under NHS contract have a statutory obligation to follow NICE guidelines.

Schedule 3(2) National Institute for Clinical Excellence guidance

14. The contractor shall provide services under the contract in accordance with any relevant guidance that is issued by the National Institute for Clinical Excellence(a), in particular the guidance entitled "Dental recall - Recall interval between routine dental examinations"(b).

NICE say they seek to promote the highest quality treatment in the NHS whilst also acting to ensure cost-effectiveness. Let us digress into a little diagram:

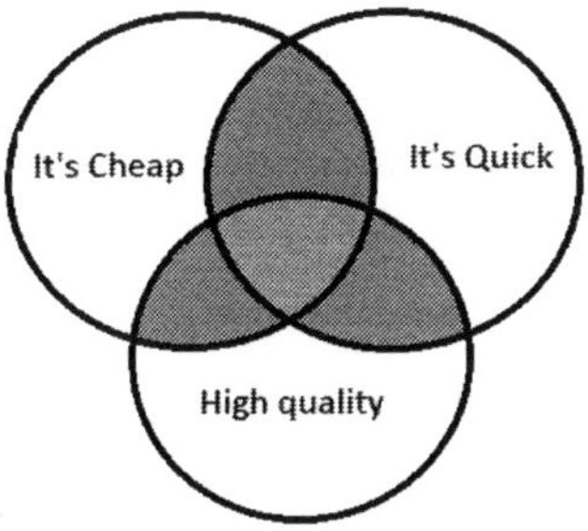

In health care you can only have two of the three. You can have cheap and high quality, but it won't be delivered quickly. You can have High Quality delivered quickly, but it won't be cheap. And you can have low cost delivered quickly, but the quality will likely be of a sub optimal nature.

But NICE is there and we have to work with it. NICE provide a heck of a lot of guidance for dentists, and I know for a fact a large percentage of NHS dentists are either ignorant of it, or ignoring it. Here are some of the topics they cover:

- **Adopt a patient-centred approach**
- **Carry out an Oral Health Review**
- **Provide Oral health advice**[20]
- **Create an individually tailored dental care plan with the patient**
- **Choose the interval before the next oral health review**[21]**.** We as dentists can both agree that anything more than 12

months is pushing the boundaries of acceptability. And yet they say it is sometimes acceptable to do 24.

- **Review the recall interval at the next oral health review**
- **They provide advice on Wisdom tooth extraction[22]**
- **They provide guidance on mini/micro screw implementation for orthodontic anchorage[23]**
- **Oh and ozone[24]**

The question is, would a private dentist need to follow the same guidance. At the end of the day, a lot of research has gone into NICE. And my flippant comment aside, it does tend to advise on the best clinical practice and provides guidelines in order to provide a uniformity in the quality of treatment across the country. As a private dentist you would perhaps be deemed as foolish for not following NICE guidelines. There are many authors and authorities that would state that you should. You would need a very strong clinical reason to not follow the guidance set out by such an esteemed national body.

HealthWatch[25]

A patient vising the Healthwatch website might perhaps not really understand what it was all about. I struggled. It is an independent organisation and reports to the CQC. Basically, it works through collecting feedback of healthcare establishments, said feedback being passed onto the CQC. Think of it a bit like TripAdvisor, with the risk that enough bad reviews would see the CQC descend upon you.

To get a clear understanding on providing NHS care, I recommend reading the book **Understanding NHS Dentistry** by Michael Watson, Raj Rattan and Len D'Cruz. It's very good.

Regulation references:

1. **Dentist Act 1984 -**
   http://www.legislation.gov.uk/ukpga/1984/24
2. **Standards for the Dental Team, GDC 2013 -**
   https://standards.gdc-uk.org/
3. **GDC supplementary guidance -**
   https://www.gdcuk.org/professionals/standards/team
4. **The General Dental Council (Fitness to Practise) Rules Order of Council 2006 -**
   http://www.legislation.gov.uk/uksi/2006/1663/schedule/made
5. **GMC publication Good Medical practice -**
   http://www.gmc-uk.org/guidance/good_medical_practice.asp
6. **Roylance v General Medical Council -**
   http://www.bailii.org/uk/cases/UKPC/1999/16.html
7. **GDC - Case Examiner Guidance Manual - 2016 -**
   https://www.gdc-uk.org/about/who-we-are/committees/case-examiners
8. **Health and Social Care Act 2008 -**
   https://www.legislation.gov.uk/ukpga/2008/14/contents
9. **How CQC Regulates: Primary care dental Services, Provider handbook. March 2015 -**

http://www.cqc.org.uk/sites/default/files/20150611_dental_care_provider_handbook.pdf

10. **CQC, The scope of registration - Registration under the Health and Social Care Act 2008 -** http://www.cqc.org.uk/sites/default/files/20151230_100001_Scope_of_registration_guidance_updated_March_2015_01.pdf
11. **CQC Notifications -** http://www.cqc.org.uk/guidance-providers/notifications/notification-finder
12. **Nigel's surgery 63: Disruption to services** – notifying CQC - http://www.cqc.org.uk/guidance-providers/gps/nigels-surgery-63-disruption-services-%E2%80%93-notifying-cqc
13. **CQC: Offences -** http://www.cqc.org.uk/guidance-providers/regulations-enforcement/offences
14. **The National Health Service (General Dental Services Contracts) Regulations 2005 -** http://www.legislation.gov.uk/uksi/2005/3361/regulation/2/made
15. **The National Health Service (Personal Dental Services Agreements) Regulations 2005 -** http://www.legislation.gov.uk/uksi/2005/3373/contents/made
16. **The National Health Service (General Dental Services Contracts) (Wales) Regulations 2006 -**

http://www.legislation.gov.uk/wsi/2006/490/contents/mad
e

17. **The National Health Service (Personal Dental Services Agreements) (Wales) Regulations 2006 -** https://www.legislation.gov.uk/wsi/2006/489/contents/ma
de
18. **The National Health Service (Dental Charges) Regulations 2005 -** https://www.legislation.gov.uk/ukdsi/2005/0110736400/c
ontents
19. **NICHE** - https://www.nice.org.uk/
20. **Provide Oral health advice -** https://www.nice.org.uk/Guidance/NG30
21. **Choose the interval before the next oral health review** - https://www.nice.org.uk/Guidance/CG19
22. **They provide advice on Wisdom tooth extraction -** https://www.nice.org.uk/guidance/TA1
23. **They provide guidance on mini/micro screw implementation for orthodontic anchorage-** https://www.nice.org.uk/guidance/IPG238
24. **Oh and ozone** - https://www.nice.org.uk/guidance/TA92
25. **Healthcare Watch** - http://www.healthwatch.co.uk/

Complaints

There is no remit in the book to discuss the actual handling of complaints. For such matter we highly recommend the Dental protection publication "**Handling Complaints**"[1] which is one of the better such publications available. Whilst it is not for me to show you how to set up a complaints system (each practice is supposed to set up their own) I can show you what is expected of you.

The GDC

Complaints are a fact of life and you need to accept it. You should not fear complaints, even in the present harsh litigious and regulatory environment. Complaints, if managed properly, are a way to turn an unhappy patient into a happy patient. You should have systems in place to handle them and handle them well. As it happens, the GDC has a lot to say on the matter of complaints. They will (unless the matter is severe) advise that the issue be raised with the dentist first, but know that the GDC have a legal obligation to investigate any and all complaints that are presented to them (we have already discussed how the FTP process works).

GDC Principle 5 - Have a clear and effective complaints procedure

5.1 You must make sure that there is an effective complaints procedure readily available for patients to use, and follow that procedure at all times

5.1.1 It is part of your responsibility as a dental professional to deal with complaints properly and professionally. You must:

- *ensure that there is an effective written complaints procedure where you work;*
- *follow the complaints procedure at all times;*
- *respond to complaints within the time limits set out in the procedure; and*
- *provide a constructive response to the complaint.*

5.1.2 You should make sure that everyone (dental professionals, other staff and patients) knows about the complaints procedure and understands how it works. If you are an employer, or you manage a team, you must ensure that all staff are trained in handling complaints.

5.1.3 If you work for a practice that provides NHS (or equivalent health service) treatment, or if you work in a hospital, you should follow the procedure set down by that organisation.

5.1.4 If you work in private practice, including private practice owned by a dental body corporate, you should make sure that it has a procedure which sets similar standards and time limits to the NHS (or equivalent health service) procedure.

5.1.5 You should make sure that your complaints procedure:

- *is displayed where patients can see it - patients should not have to ask for a copy;*
- *is clearly written in plain language and is*
- *available in other formats if needed;*
- *is easy for patients to understand and follow;*
- *provides information on other independent organisations that patients can contact to raise concerns;*

- *allows you to deal with complaints promptly and efficiently;*
- *allows you to investigate complaints in a full and fair way;*
- *explains the possible outcomes; allows information that can be used to improve services to pass back to your practice management or equivalent and respects patients' confidentiality.*

5.1.6 Complaints can be an opportunity to improve your service. You should analyse any complaints that you receive to help you improve the service you offer, and share lessons learnt from complaints with all team members.

5.1.7 You should keep a written record of all complaints together with your responses. This record should be separate from your patient records so that patients are not discouraged from making a complaint. You should use your record of complaints to monitor your performance in handling complaints and identify any areas that need to be improved.

5.2 You must respect a patient's right to complain

5.2.1 You should not react defensively to complaints. You should listen carefully to patients who complain and involve them fully in the complaints process. You should find out what outcome patients want from their complaint.

5.3 You must give patients who complain a prompt and constructive response Guidance

5.3.1 You should give the patient a copy of the complaints procedure when you acknowledge their complaint so that they understand the stages involved and the timescales.

5.3.2 You should deal with complaints in a calm and constructive way and in line with the complaints procedure.

5.3.3 You should aim to resolve complaints as efficiently, effectively and politely as possible.

5.3.4 You must respond to complaints within the time limits set out in your complaints procedure.

5.3.5 If you need more time to investigate a complaint, you should tell the patient when you will respond.

5.3.6 If there are exceptional circumstances which mean that the complaint cannot be resolved within the usual timescale, you should give the patient regular updates (at least every 10 days) on progress.

5.3.7 You should try to deal with all the points raised in the complaint and, where possible, offer a solution for each one.

5.3.8 You should offer an apology and a practical solution where appropriate.

5.3.9 If a complaint is justified, you should offer a fair solution. This may include offering to put things right at your own expense if you have made a mistake.

5.3.10 You should respond to the patient in writing, setting out your findings and any practical solutions you are prepared to offer. Make sure that the letter is clear, deals with the patient's concerns and is easy for them to understand.

5.3.11 If the patient is not satisfied despite your best efforts to resolve their complaint, you should tell them about other avenues that are open to them, such as the relevant Ombudsman for health service complaints or the Dental Complaints Service for complaints about private treatment.

So ask yourselves a few questions. Is your complaints procedure in compliance with all that and is it displayed prominently? If you discourage complaints, you will leave patients with little recourse other than to go to either a lawyer or the GDC…perhaps both.

Dental Complaints Service (DCS)[2]

A few years back, the GDC was criticised by dentists for the way in which they advertised this valuable service to the public. Some of you may remember the adverts in the London papers. Whilst the wording of the advert (that you paid for) left a lot to be desired, in hindsight I actually support what they were trying to do.

The DCS is free to patients, impartial and acts as a form of mediation. Although it is funded by the GDC, it considers itself to be independent from them, and can often act as a buffer that stops a patient going down the litigation or regulatory road. The process is as follows:

The patient contacts the DCS, at which point they will advise bringing the matter up with you if not done so already. If the patients aren't happy with your response to their complaint, the DCS complaints officers will work with the patient and dentist to reach a resolution. If said resolution is not forthcoming, the matter can be put before an advisory panel (two lay members

and a dentist) who will work towards an agreement and make recommendations to try and resolve the complaint.

It is thought that the advice of an independent panel can sometimes encourage reason on behalf of both sides. There is of course nothing to stop the patient taking the matter further, but many people just want to have their side of the story heard and understood by the other party.

Parliamentary and Health Service Ombudsman (PHSO)[3]

The powers of the PHSO are set out in the **Parliamentary Commissioner Act 1967**[4] and the **Health Service Commissioners Act 1993**[5]. The PHSO is not part of government, nor are they a regulator or consumer champion.

The PHSO has the power to investigate a complaint made against an NHS dentist by a patient. They have no powers to investigate a private dentist. Unfortunately, (or fortunately depending on your point of view) it would appear that the PHSO has no teeth. It can propose a remedy to answer the patient's complaint, but it cannot compel a dentist to adhere to its findings. That being said, how would a dentist defend not adhering to a PHSO ruling before the GDC or other regulatory body? The advice therefore is to seek your indemnifier's help if faced with such an investigation.

The Ombudsman has their own advice on how they expect you to handle complaints[7].

CQC

The CQC[7] have the same general opinion regarding complaints as the GDC. They will, in the first instance, recommend the patient contact the practice first if not already done so. My own experience (as someone complaining) with the CQC is that they are slow to respond to complaints. If the CQC accept a complaint, it could trigger an inspection or a referral of the matter to another agency such as the NHS or GDC.

16.—

1) Any complaint received must be investigated and necessary and proportionate action must be taken in response to any failure identified by the complaint or investigation.

2) The registered person must establish and operate effectively an accessible system for identifying, receiving, recording, handling and responding to complaints by service users and other persons in relation to the carrying on of the regulated activity.

3) The registered person must provide to the Commission, when requested to do so and by no later than 28 days beginning on the day after receipt of the request, a summary of—

> ***a) complaints made under such complaints system,***
>
> ***b) responses made by the registered person to such complaints and any further correspondence with the complainants in relation to such complaints, and***
>
> ***c)any other relevant information in relation to such complaints as the Commission may request.***

The NHS

The NHS has its own complaints system which is governed by the statutory instrument **NHS Complaints regulations 2009**[8]. This obliged dentists working under NHS contract to have arrangements in place to deal with NHS complaints. These regulations state that (it's a long list so bear with me):

- ***The dental practice must have procedures so complaints are dealt with efficiently so that a response can be given in a timely manner. All such information must be available to patients. These procedures must be monitored and audited to ensure they are working.***
- ***You must inform complainants that there are organisations able to help them in their complaint, for example PALS.***
- ***Dentists and their staff must deal with the complaint in a professional and courteous manner.***
- ***There must be a record of all complaints. For some reason this record must be kept external to the clinical notes as there is a fear the presence of a complaint may prejudice the dentist against the patient.***
- ***Patients must be informed of the outcome of your investigations***
- ***There must be procedures in place to act on the findings of any complaint***
- ***One of the principal dentists must be the "Responsible Person". This is the person who ensures everything is done by the book. They also are responsible for ensuring change is implemented if a complaint highlights a deficiency.***
- ***Believe it or not there must also be a designated complaints manager, the identity of this individual being shared with patients. If you are the lucky person who***

has the honour of being the "Responsible Person", you can also be the complaints manager.

- *Whilst it is usually only patients who can complain, other people can too (for example carers, parents etc). If such a complaint arises the "Responsible Person" needs to decide if the complaint is in the best interest of the person they are complaining for. If you don't think they are, you must write to them and tell them why.*
- *The patient does not have to complain to the practice in the first instance, and can go straight to the Local Area Team, who will inform the practice regarding the complaint.*
- *The complaint should be dealt with in a timely fashion.*
- *If you offer to discuss the complaint with the patient, and that offer is declined you must document this and write to the patient telling them how you intend to proceed.*
- *If someone complains to you verbally and you deal with it within 24 hours to the patient's satisfaction, it doesn't come under the regulations*
- *All other complaints (including those made orally) must be responded to within 3 working days. Although you are allowed to respond orally, best to do so in writing as well so there is a paper trail. If the patient complains orally, you must make a written record of that complaint and give the patient a copy.*
- *If you have concluded your investigation you must write and tell the patient your findings, including how you went about investigating the complaint. The Responsible Person should sign the letter. If the complaint has not been resolved and if you feel nothing more can be done at this local level, the letter should tell the patient what their further options are, such as taking the matter to the Ombudsman, GDC etc.*

- ***As with all bureaucracy you should make an annual declaration to the LAT about the number of complaints you receive. They will usually email you a pro-former to fill out every year.***

There is specific guidance provided by the DOH in this regard, specifically the 2009 DOH document "**Listening, responding, improving: a guide to better customer care**"[9] If you haven't read it, we strongly recommend that you do.

The way complaints are dealt with are also outlined in the 2006 NHS contract legislation (but this must be adjusted where necessary to take into account the 2009 NHS complaints legislation and individual contracts, some of which were updated 2013). It still amazes me that, to this day, a large percentage of dentists have never actually read their contract from cover to cover, especially the associates who are governed by it (so I include it here for your delectation and delight with a few comments of my own). From the legislation:

Schedule 3, PART 6

COMPLAINTS

<u>Complaints procedure</u>

47.—(1) The contractor (the practice principal) ***shall establish and operate a complaints procedure to deal with any complaints in relation to any matter reasonably connected with the provision of services under the contract which shall comply with the requirements of paragraphs 48 to 50 and 52.***

(2) The contractor shall take reasonable steps to ensure that patients are aware of?

(a) the complaints procedure;

(b) the role of the Primary Care Trust and other bodies in relation to complaints about services under the contract; and

(c) their right to assistance with any complaint from independent advocacy services provided under section 19A of the Act(c) (independent advocacy services).

(3) The contractor shall take reasonable steps to ensure that the complaints procedure is accessible to all patients (Define reasonable?).

Making of complaints

48.—(1) A complaint may be made by or, with his consent, on behalf of a patient or former patient, who is receiving or has received services under the contract, or:

(a) where the patient is a child, by:

(i) a parent;

(ii) a person duly authorised by a local authority to whose care the child has been committed under the provisions of the Children Act 1989(d); or

(iii) a person duly authorised by a voluntary organisation by which the child is being accommodated under the provisions of that Act; or

(b) where the patient is incapable of making a complaint, by a relative or other adult person who has an interest in his welfare.

(2) Where a patient has died, a complaint may be made by a relative or other adult person who had an interest in his welfare or, where the patient falls within sub-paragraph (1)(a)(ii) or (iii) by the authority or a voluntary organisation.

Period for making complaints

49.—(1) Subject to sub-paragraph (2), the period for making a complaint is:

> ***(a) six months beginning with the date on which the matter which is the subject of the complaint occurred; or***
>
> ***(b) six months beginning with the date on which the matter which is the subject of the complaint comes to the complainant's notice provided that the complaint is made no later than 12 months after the date on which the matter which is the subject of the complaint occurred.***

(2) Where a complaint is not made during the period specified in sub-paragraph (1), it shall be referred to the person nominated under paragraph 50(2)(a) and if he is of the opinion that:

> ***(a) having regard to all the circumstances of the case, it would have been unreasonable for the complainant to make the complaint within that period; and***
>
> ***(b) notwithstanding the time that has elapsed since the date on which the matter which is the subject matter of the complaint occurred, it is still possible to investigate the complaint properly, the complaint shall be treated as if it had been received during the period specified in sub-paragraph (1).*** (A complaint is unlikely to go away just because it falls outside these time parameters)

Further requirements for complaints procedures

50.—(1) A complaints procedure shall also comply with the requirements set out in sub-paragraphs (2) to (6).

(2) The contractor must nominate

(a) a person (who need not be connected with the contractor and who, in the case of an individual, may be specified by his job title) to be responsible for the operation of the complaints procedure and the investigation of complaints; and

(b) a partner, or other senior person associated with the contractor, to be responsible for the effective management of the complaints procedure and for ensuring that action is taken in the light of the outcome of any investigation.

(3) All complaints must be:

(a) either made or recorded in writing; (all verbal complaints must be recorded)

(b) acknowledged in writing within the period of three working days beginning with the day on which the complaint was made or, where that is not possible, as soon as reasonably practicable; and

(c) properly investigated.

(4) Within the period of ten working days beginning with the day on which the complaint was received by the person specified under sub-paragraph (2)(a) or, where that is not possible, as soon as reasonably practicable, the complainant must be given a written summary of the investigation and its conclusions.

(5) Where the investigation of the complaint requires consideration of the patient's dental records, the person

specified in sub-paragraph (2)(a) must inform the patient or person acting on his behalf if the investigation will involve disclosure of information contained in those records to a person other than the contractor or an employee of the contractor.

(6) The contractor must keep a record of all complaints and copies of all correspondence relating to complaints for a period of at least two years from the date on which such complaints were made, but such records shall be kept separate from patients' dental records.

Co-operation with investigations

51.—(1) The contractor shall co-operate with—

(a) any investigation of a complaint in relation to any matter reasonably connected with the provision of services under the contract undertaken by—

(i) the Primary Care Trust; and

(ii) the Commission for Healthcare Audit and Inspection; and

(b) any investigation of a complaint by an NHS body or local authority which relates to a patient or former patient of the contractor.

(2) In sub-paragraph (1)— "NHS body" means a Primary Care Trust, an NHS trust, an NHS foundation trust, a Strategic Health "NHS body" means a Primary Care Trust, an NHS trust, an NHS foundation trust, a Strategic Health

Authority, a Local Health Board, a Health Board, a Health and Social Services Board, a Health and Social Services Trust or, a Health Board or Special Health Board constituted under section 2 of the National Health Service (Scotland) Act 1978(a); "local authority" means—

(a) any of the bodies listed in section 1 of the Local Authority Social Services Act 1970(b) (local authorities);

(b) the Council of the Isles of Scilly; or

(c) a council constituted under section 2 of the Local Government etc. (Scotland) Act 1994(c) (constitution of councils).

(3) The co-operation required by sub-paragraph (1) includes—

(a) answering questions reasonably put to the contractor by the Primary Care Trust;

(b) providing any information relating to the complaint reasonably required by the Primary Care Trust; and

(c) attending any meeting to consider the complaint (if held at a reasonably accessible place and at a reasonable hour, and due notice has been given) if the contractor's presence at the meeting is reasonably required by the Primary Care Trust.

Provision of information

52. The contractor shall inform the Primary Care Trust, at such intervals as the Primary Care Trust requires, of the number of complaints it has received under the procedure established in accordance with this Part.

NHS complaints can range from unfavourable comments on NHS choices, poor ratings on the Friends and Family Test[11] all the way to full blown investigations. They can complain to you, the dentist, or to the local NHS commissioner directly by emailing **england.contactus@nhs.net** with "For the attention of the complaints team" in the subject line. It's literally as easy as that for them.

Complaints about secondary care are either made to the hospital involved or the Clinical Commissioning Group (CCG)[12]. If the NHS does choose to investigate a complaint, the pathway they will follow can be found in the NHS document "**Toolkit for Managing Performance Concerns in primary Care**"[13]. If you work in the NHS and you haven't read that, then you know what you need to do.

Whilst I would like to go into this in depth, please understand it is a 70-page document. I will summarise what sanction the NHS can decide on however. At the time of writing, when it comes to primary care, complaints can be referred to a "**Performers List Decision panel**" or PDLP. For a primary care NHS performer this is no laughing matter, because your ability to provide NHS care depends on you having a performer number and being on the list of approved dentists. The PDLP have five decision they can make under the 2013 Performer List Regulations (which is a statutory instrument)[13].

- **Take no action**
- **Suspend you as an NHS performer**
- **Place conditions on your provision of NHS care**
- **Remove you from the performer list**
- **Refuse to include you in the list if you apply**

So yes, the NHS complaints system, which many dentists don't seem to understand, is not to be ignored.

General comments

Strangely enough, the principles and the concepts laid out by the NHS complaints system may also apply to private practice as well. At the very least, a private practice will be expected to have something comparable. Most plan schemes have their own complaints procedure which dentists must follow, and do remember that, when it comes to monthly payment plans, you have entered into a contract with your patient.

Is it better if the patients don't complain? Some dentists would think so, but I do not. Some patients don't want to cause a fuss, they just wander off to another practice or another dentist. And how are you supposed to learn and grow if that happens? Sometimes the complaint isn't about you personally, but about the practice itself. This is why most large companies now ask for feedback when you use their services. That culture is now so pervasive that to some of us it can seem onerous. They know that happy customers return, and that unhappy ones go away and grumble and moan about your business to the multitudes.

Sometimes it is better FOR a patient to complain than it is for them to go elsewhere, especially if the issue is about the quality of the work you have done. Do you want them coming to you, or to the GDC? Do you want to fix the problem or do you want one of the ever growing number of hyper critical dentists telling the patient how shocking they think your work is?

Even better than a complaining patient is a happy patient. To keep the patient on side and to stop these complaints from happening you need to create a culture in your practice that the patients can sense. A culture that promotes excellence, honesty and trust, where patients see that their care is the most important thing. Do the job well in a compassionate and ethical manner.

I have perhaps a controversial view on this. Would you have expected anything less? I welcome feedback and complaints when they are valid. The valid is an important caveat because some people like to complain, and those rare individuals are sometimes not the right people for your practice. Of course, as this is a book regarding law and regulation, it is important to say that such peoples' complaints should not be ignored.

That being said, I would hope that the experienced amongst you would, by now, have developed systems in your practice to attract the kinds of people you want to treat. In a nutshell, as a primary care provider, you should only treat patients that you like/respect and that you are in rapport with. This is the controversial bit, and it's purely MY OPINION. It in no way constitutes advice. Invariably however a large percentage of the people who cause a "a right royal ruckus" are the ones you had reservations about whilst you were treating them.

As we age as professionals, most of us develop a little voice in the back of our heads that tells us when we perhaps shouldn't be starting on a treatment path with certain individuals. This is almost always in the patient's best interests, because when you invite those you have reservations about to seek their dental care elsewhere, they invariably end up with a dentist who is more in tune with their psychology. You cannot treat everybody, and you shouldn't even try to.

Why not create an environment to attract the types of patients you want to treat? That way, when that rare and justified complaint arises, you can use it as a valid opportunity to grow as a dentist and as a practice. Many practices don't do this. They see all and sundry without any type of selection process (one that in no way discriminates in any way) and then wonder why the practice is full of patients who do not seem to value and appreciate the dentistry on offer.

A practice complaint procedure must

- ***Be straightforward***
- ***allow you to deal with complaints promptly and efficiently***
- ***allow you to investigate complaints in a full and fair way***
- ***allow information that can be used to improve services to pass back to your practice management or equivalent and respects patients' confidentiality***
- ***be freely available and***
    - i. ***be clearly written in plain language***
    - ii. ***be easy for patients to understand and follow***
    - iii. ***include time limits so that patients know how long the process may take***
    - iv. ***explain the possible outcomes***
    - v. ***include information on other independent organisations that patients can contact to raise concerns***
    - vi. ***be available in other formats if needed.***

If you are an NHS practice, your complaints procedure must conform to the NHS model. DPL[14] do a very good guide on complaints handling.

Complaints References:

1. **DPL: Handling Complaints:** http://www.dentalprotection.org/docs/librariesprovider4/dental-advice-booklets/dental-advice-booklet-complaints-handling-england.pdf?sfvrsn=36
2. **Dental Complaints Service (DCS** - https://dcs.gdc-uk.org/
3. **Parliamentary and Health Service Ombudsman (PHSO)** - https://www.ombudsman.org.uk/
4. **Parliamentary Commissioner Act 1967** - http://www.legislation.gov.uk/ukpga/1967/13/introduction
5. **Health Service Commissioners Act 1993 -** http://www.legislation.gov.uk/ukpga/1993/46/contents
6. **Parliamentary and Health Service Ombudsman: Principles of complaint handling -** https://www.ombudsman.org.uk/about-us/our-principles/principles-good-complaint-handling
7. **CQC Regulation 16: Receiving and acting on complaints** - http://www.cqc.org.uk/guidance-providers/regulations-enforcement/regulation-16-receiving-acting-complaints
8. **NHS Complaints regulations 2009 -** http://www.legislation.gov.uk/uksi/2009/309/contents/made
9. **DOH "Listening, responding, improving: a guide to better customer care" -** http://webarchive.nationalarchives.gov.uk/20130104082528/http://www.dh.gov.uk/en/Publicationsandstatistics/Publications/PublicationsPolicyAndGuidance/DH_095408
10. **Friends and Family Test** - https://www.england.nhs.uk/ourwork/pe/fft/

11. **Clinical Commissioning Group (CCG)** - http://www.nhs.uk/Service-Search/Clinical-Commissioning-Group/LocationSearch/1
12. **Toolkit for Managing Performance Concerns in primary Care** - https://www.england.nhs.uk/wp-content/uploads/2016/02/toolkit-managing-performance-concerns-pc-feb16.pdf
13. **Performer List Regulations 2013** - http://www.legislation.gov.uk/uksi/2013/335/contents/made
14. **DPL: Complaints Handling** - https://www.dentalprotection.org/docs/librariesprovider4/dental-advice-booklets/dental-advice-booklet-complaints-handling-england.pdf

Confidentiality

There is a statutory requirement for medical personnel to disclose confidential medical information about certain individuals in specific scenarios. For example, see the guidance from the General Medical Council **Confidentiality: Reporting gunshot and knife wounds**[1]. Section 172 of the **1988 Road Traffic Act**[2] also instils an obligation on dentists to provide information which may help in identifying a driver in an RTA. Such examples are not perhaps relevant to the busy GDP, but you need to be aware of these rare laws and regulations. If this statutory requirement does not exist, then in most instances the competent adult would need to be asked for their consent to share their information onto a third party.

Patients, on the whole, have the right for their details and their dental records to be kept secret. No longer is it acceptable to joke about Mrs Miggins and her relentlessly loose upper full denture in the pub after work. Patients rightly expect and demand that their details and their affairs be kept secret from those who have no business knowing anything about them. And the lawyers and the regulators will hold us in poor regard if we, as professionals, breach our patients trust in this matter. So important is it, the GDC have a whole Principle dedicated to it, Principle 4, which we shall discuss in a moment. They did at one time produce a specific advice sheet, but at the occasion of writing, it does not seem to be presently available.

Unfortunately running a dental practice makes it very difficult to keep confidentiality 100% of the time. In the coming chapter I will go over the law of confidentiality and hopefully show you how difficult the whole topic is. Perhaps one of the best guides on the subject is the one produced by Dental Protection Ltd (DPL again?) called **Confidentiality**[3]. It is feely available, and if you haven't already done so, I strongly advise you read it.

From what follows we will try and decipher three things

1) What information is classed as confidential (what, for example is a Health Record?)

2) How to release information with the patient's express permission

3) When information can be released without the consent of the patient

Your ethical obligation

You have an ethical obligation to maintain confidentiality. To me the ethical obligation should be self-evident but some people do need reminding about ethics from time to time. Not everyone in our profession holds their ethical duty to the high standards expected by the majority of us. And there will be times when your ethical duty will be tested. As sad as it is to say however, the ethical obligation perhaps comes second to your legal and regulatory obligation.

Your regulatory obligation

GDC

As already stated, registration comes with an obligation to follow the rules laid out by the GDC, otherwise known as the standards which I now reproduce for your viewing pleasure. A failure to maintain confidentiality can result in a complaint to the GDC, which as I am sure you will agree is a very serious matter.

4.2 You must protect the confidentiality of patients' information and only use it for the purpose for which it was given

4.2.1 Confidentiality is central to the relationship and trust between you and your patients. You must keep patient information confidential. This applies to all the information about patients that you have learnt in your professional role including personal details, medical history, what treatment they are having and how much it costs.

4.2.2 You must ensure that non-registered members of the dental team are aware of the importance of confidentiality and that they keep patient information confidential at all times.

4.2.3 You must not post any information or comments about patients on social networking or blogging sites. If you use professional social media to discuss anonymised cases for the purpose of discussing best practice you must be careful that the patient or patients cannot be identified. See our website for further guidance on social networking.

4.2.4 You must not talk about patients or their treatment in places where you can be overheard by people who should not have access to the information you are discussing.

4.2.5 You must explain to patients the circumstances in which you may need to share information with others involved in their healthcare. This includes making sure that they understand:

- ***what information you will be releasing;***
- ***why you will be releasing it; and***
- ***the likely consequences of you releasing the information.***

You must give your patients the opportunity to withhold their permission to share information in this way unless exceptional

circumstances apply. You must record in your patient's notes whether or not they gave their permission.

4.2.6 If a patient allows you to share information about them, you <u>should</u> ensure that anyone you share it with understands that it is confidential.

4.2.7 If other people ask you to provide information about patients (for example, for teaching or research), or if you want to use patient information such as photographs for any reason, you <u>must</u>:

- ***explain to patients how the information or images will be used;***
- ***check that patients understand what they are agreeing to;***
- ***obtain and record the patients' consent to their use;***
- ***only release or use the minimum information necessary for the purpose; and***
- ***explain to the patients that they can withdraw their permission at any time.***
- ***If it is not necessary for patients to be identified, you must make sure they remain anonymous in any information you release.***

4.2.8 You <u>must</u> keep patient information confidential even after patients die.

4.2.9 The duty to keep information confidential also covers recordings or images of patients such as photographs, videos or audio recordings, both originals and copies, including those made on a mobile phone. You <u>must</u> not make any recordings or images without the patient's permission.

<u>4.3 You must only release a patient's information without their permission in exceptional circumstances</u>

4.3.1 In exceptional circumstances, you may be justified in releasing confidential patient information without their consent if doing so is in the best interests of the public or the patient. This could happen if a patient puts their own safety or that of others at serious risk, or if information about a patient could be important in preventing or detecting a serious crime.

If you believe that revealing information about a patient is in the best interests of the public or the patient, you should first try to get the patient's permission to release the information. You should do everything you can to encourage the patient to either release the information themselves or to give you permission to do so. You must document the efforts you have made to obtain consent in the patient's notes.

4.3.2 If obtaining consent from a patient to the release of their information in the public interest is not practical or appropriate, or if the patient will not give their permission, you should get advice from your defence organisation or professional association before you release the information.

4.3.3 If you have information that a patient is or could be at risk of significant harm, or you suspect that a patient is a victim of abuse, you must inform the appropriate social care agencies or the police. See our website for further guidance.

4.3.4 You can be ordered by a court, or you can be under a statutory duty, to release information about a patient without their permission. If this happens, you should only release the minimum amount of information necessary to comply with the court order or statutory duty.

4.3.5 In any circumstance where you decide to release confidential information, you must document your reasons and be prepared to explain and justify your decision and actions.

I want to take a moment, if I may, to share a few thoughts about this guidance to see if it "makes sense" in the modern world.

4.2.3 talks about Social media. It might be worth reading that Standard again. The Standard doesn't say you are allowed to get patient's consent to put their information on Social media. The Standard clearly states you must not do so. There is no grey area here if we go by the Standard alone. Is a Facebook group classed as professional social media? Probably not

However, there is clarity in the GDC's document "**Guidance on Using Social media**"[4]. This therefore displays the importance behind reading ALL the guidance issued

You must be careful not to share identifiable information about patients without their explicit consent. When obtaining consent, you should specify to the patient how exactly the information you propose to share will be used, for what purpose and where it will be available.

If you are sharing anonymised patient information, you must also take all possible precautions to make sure that the patient cannot be identified. Although individual pieces of information may not breach a patient's confidentiality on their own, a number of pieces of patient information published online could be enough to identify them or someone close to them

Next, when we read **4.2.5**, think about what that means for a second. It means, for example, that you should get your patient's explicit permission to send their impression to the laboratory. You must record in your patient's notes whether or not they gave their permission.

Appendix 3 shows a model patient consent form, which outlines the guidance **in 4.2.7**. How many on Facebook are doing all of this do you think? And how do you remove those photos from Facebook at a later date should the patient come back and object? My advice is don't post on social media at all, but if you must, only post anonymous images on Social Media, because anything else may come back to haunt you and the patient. As an example of this, there is a social media site called 9gag, where people post images and other people comment on those images. One such post consisted of a before and after full face pictures of a child orthodontic patient. Some of the comments were quite disparaging and heart rending. I can guarantee that no parent would have given their consent for their child's images to be used if they had known that such a thing would have occurred.

4.3.1 tells us that if you believe revealing information about a patient is in the best interests of the public or the patient you should first try to get the patient's permission to release that information. You should do everything you can to encourage the patient to either release the information themselves or to give you permission to do so. You must document the efforts you have made to obtain consent in the patient's notes…… you will notice that this is a "should" not a "must". That's because there will be occasions where the safety of the patient/public has precedence, in which case you should seek the advice of your indemnifier. The GDC then go on to say that if you have information that a patient is or could be at risk of significant harm, or you suspect that a patient is a victim of abuse, you must inform the appropriate social care agencies or the police. You do not have a choice in this.

The document **Confidentiality: NHS Code of Practice**[5] describes the public interest as:

"Exceptional circumstances that justify overruling the right of an individual to confidentiality in order to serve the broader social interest. Decisions about the public interest are complex and must take account of both the potential harm that disclosure may cause and the interest of society in the continued provision of confidential health services".

Under what scenarios can patient's information be released without permission?

Usually only in exceptional circumstances. If the patient puts their safety or the safety of others at risk, or if the information you provide could help prevent a serious crime. You should ideally contact your defence agency first though.

CQC

The CQC also expect you to keep information confidential. Confidentiality and privacy are mentioned in several of their regulations. Let us highlight where that is the case:

***Regulation 15(1)(c)* - "Premises must be fit for purpose.....making sure privacy, dignity and confidentiality are not compromised".**

***Regulation 16(2)* - "Consent and Confidentiality must not be compromised during the complaints process".**

***Regulation 17(2)(a)* - "Subject to statutory consent and applicable confidentiality requirements, providers must share relevant information....with other relevant bodies."**

***Regulation 17(2)(c)* -**

- ***"Be accessible to authorised people as necessary in order to deliver people's care and treatment in a way that meets their needs and keeps them safe. This applies both internally and externally to other organisations.***

- *Be created, amended, stored and destroyed in line with current legislation and nationally recognised guidance.*
- *Be kept secure at all times and only accessed, amended, or securely destroyed by authorised people.*
- *Both paper and electronic records can be held securely providing they meet the requirements of the Data Protection Act 1998.*
- *Decisions made on behalf of a person who lacks capacity must be recorded and provide evidence that these have been taken in line with the requirements of the Mental Capacity Act 2005 or, where relevant, the Mental Health Act 1983, and their associated Codes of Practice.*
- *Information in all formats must be managed in line with current legislation and guidance.*
- *Systems and processes must support the confidentiality of people using the service and not contravene the Data Protection Act 1998."*

Regulation 17(2)(d) -

- *Records relating to people employed and the management of regulated activities must be created, amended, stored and destroyed in accordance with*

  current legislation and guidance.

- *Records relating to people employed (remember that confidentiality isn't just about patient's) must include information relevant to their employment in the role including information relating to the requirements under Regulations 4 to 7 and Regulation 19 of this part (part 3) of the Health and Social Care Act 2008 (Regulated Activities) Regulations 2014. This applies to all staff, not just newly appointed staff. Providers must*

observe data protection legislation about the retention of confidential personal information.

- ***Records must be kept secure at all times and only accessed, amended or destroyed by people who are authorised to do so.***
- ***Information in all formats must be managed in line with current legislation and guidance.***
- ***Systems and processes must support the confidentiality of people using the service and not contravene the Data Protection Act 1998.***

So there's not actually that much on Confidentiality that hasn't already been said, but as is the way with bureaucrats, they also use the word Privacy. So what does the CQC say about privacy?

10(2)(a) - Ensure the privacy of service users

> ***"This insures making sure that people have privacy when they need and want it…"***
> ***"Each person's privacy must be maintained at all times…."***
> ***"Staff must ensure that people have privacy when they receive treatment…"***
> ***"Each person's privacy needs and expectations should be identified, recorded, and met as far as is reasonably possible."***

15(1)(c) - already covered above

So from a regulatory stand point, the CQC are not one to worry too much about.

Your legal obligation

Confidentiality can be set aside by legislation in certain circumstances. When it comes to legislation and confidentiality it is perhaps prudent to deal with all legislation that covers the collection, retention, disposal and disclosure of confidential information. There are 4 main Acts of Parliament that cover health records. The Data Protection Act, the Access to health records Act, the Freedom of Information Act and the Access to Medical Reports Act. There is also other legislation which we shall cover. Then of course there is the GDPR.

The DOH have produced a useful guide that covers these acts called the "**Guidance for Access to health Records Requests**"[6].

General Data Protection Regulation (GDPR)

This is an attempt by the EU to strengthen the data protection for all individuals within the EU. This will supersede the Data Protection Act...although only Satan and all his little Wizards knows what will happen come Brexit. It came into force pm May 25th 2018.

When it comes into effect, you (the data controller) must ensure personal data is processed lawfully, and said data must be discarded when no longer needed. There will be definite changes to how you get consent for the use of patient information under the GDPR. GDPR is a complicated topic and this is not the correct medium to discuss it. The implications of GDPR are too big to be covered in this book.

See **Appendix 13** for a GDP Checklist.

The **Data Protection Act**[7] **1998**(DPA) set out the principles that dentists has to follow with regards patient data and only applied to living individuals. Patient information, be it clinical or administrative, has to be accurately created, securely stored and, should the need arise, disposed of appropriately. This means that only people who had a right of access should be able to access the records as and when they need them.

The 1998 Act has been superseded by the 2018 version of the Data Protection Act and the GDPR. Much of the 2018 Act now appears to not be relevant to this discussion. Therefore, we will concentrate on the GDPR.

Basically the GDPR outlines six data protection principles that organisaiton must follow. This applies to the processing, collecting and storing of individuals' personal data. The following can be found on the ICO website at **https://ico.org.uk/for-organisations/guide-to-the-general-data-protection-regulation-gdpr/**

The six principles of the GDPR are:

1) Lawfulness, fairness and transparency:
This is to make sure you don't break the law or try and hide anything from your data subjects

- You must identify valid grounds under the GDPR (known as a 'lawful basis') for collecting and using personal data.
- You must ensure that you do not do anything with the data in breach of any other laws.
- You must use personal data in a way that is fair. This means you must not process the data in a way that is unduly detrimental, unexpected or misleading to the individuals concerned.

- You must be clear, open and honest with people from the start about how you will use their personal data.

2) Purpose limitation:
You can only collect data for a specific purpose, state what this purpose is and hold the data only so long as is required.

- You must be clear about what your purposes for processing are from the start.
- You need to record your purposes as part of your documentation obligations and specify them in your privacy information for individuals.
- You can only use the personal data for a new purpose if either this is compatible with your original purpose, you get consent, or you have a clear basis in law.

3) Data Minimisation
You must ensure the personal data you are processing is:
- adequate – sufficient to properly fulfil your stated purpose;
- relevant – has a rational link to that purpose; and
- limited to what is necessary – you do not hold more than you need for that purpose.

4) Accuracy
Every reasonable step should be taken to erase or fix data that is inaccurate/incomplete.

- You should take all reasonable steps to ensure the personal data you hold is not incorrect or misleading as to any matter of fact.
- You may need to keep the personal data updated, although this will depend on what you are using it for.

- If you discover that personal data is incorrect or misleading, you must take reasonable steps to correct or erase it as soon as possible.
- You must carefully consider any challenges to the accuracy of personal data.

5) Storage Limitation

Get rid of data when you no longer need it (there are other pieces of legislation that cover the retention of medical records):

- You must not keep personal data for longer than you need it.
- You need to think about – and be able to justify – how long you keep personal data. This will depend on your purposes for holding the data.
- You need a policy setting standard retention periods wherever possible, to comply with documentation requirements.
- You should also periodically review the data you hold, and erase or anonymise it when you no longer need it.
- You must carefully consider any challenges to your retention of data. Individuals have a right to erasure if you no longer need the data.
- You can keep personal data for longer if you are only keeping it for public interest archiving, scientific or historical research, or statistical purposes.

You might find the ICO records management checklist useful:

https://ico.org.uk/for-organisations/resources-and-support/data-protection-self-assessment/records-management-checklist/

6) Integrity and confidentiality (security)
You have to protect and keep confidential the data you store.

7) Accountability
You need to take responsibility for what you do with personal data and how you comply with the other principles.

You must have appropriate measures and records in place to be able to demonstrate your compliance with all these principles.

Just so you know, it can be a criminal offence to breach the GDPR, with stiff penalties. I only only been able to discuss GDPR in the very broadest terms as it is highly complex and beyond the scope of this book.

Access to Health Records Act 1990[9]

The meaning of a health professional in this act is the same as under the Data Protection Act. Confidentiality obligations owed by health professionals continue after death, and this Act gives certain individuals the right to apply for access to deceased person's records, specifically as seen in Section 3(1)(f) the "*patient's personal representative and any person who may have a claim arising out of the patient's death*". Applicants should provide evidence of their right to access, and it is strongly advised that, should a claim arise, you put the matter in the hands of your indemnifier. This Act also gives a definition of the term "health records" which is similar to that in the DPA. A health record is a record that

"a) consists of information relating to the physical or mental health of an individual who can be identified from the

information or from that and other information in the possession of the holder of the record; and

b) has been made by or on behalf of a health professional in connection with the care of that individual"

A request for access should be made in writing and with evidence. Once you are satisfied that the person requesting access had the right to view the notes, you should comply with the request within **40 days** (or 21 days for a part of the record that was added within the last 40 days).

You are also allowed to charge a fee for access which needs to be paid up front. I am informed that the 40-day time limit applies from when the required information and fee are provided.

- Viewing of physical record - **FOC**
- Viewing of physical record where an entry has been added in the last 40 days - **£10**
- Viewing records held wholly or partially on computer - **£10**
- Hard copies of records - **No limit on the fee**, but the record holder is not allowed to profit from the procedure. This fee is additional to the initial £10 for access

Should the records indicate that the deceased wished the information to remain confidential then it should not be disclosed unless there is an overriding public interest in disclosing. So that would be time for your indemnifier again. Make them earn their money ☺

Freedom of Information Act 2000[10]

The Freedom of Information Act (FOIA) gives patients the right to ask any public authorities (as well as those who supply services to public authorities) for all the information they have on any subject they choose. This is a much ignored act by dentists, and it shouldn't be. Whilst most dental practices are not public authorities (as stipulated in the 2006 contract) they often do provide services to public authorities, namely NHS England through the Area Teams and arguable the NHS Business Services Authority. Therefore if a request is made to a dental practice with an NHS contract, they would be obliged to release information related to the NHS work.

This is not to say you can just write in to any old dental practice and find out how many times Mrs Miggins has lost her denture. The FOI is not intended to allow people to gain access to private sensitive information about themselves or others, such as information held in health records. Those wishing to access personal information about themselves should apply under the Dental Protection Act. Health records of the deceased are also exempt under the FOIA. Therefore, information that could be classed as a health record is exempt from the FOIA. Also information that is given in confidence is exempt.

The ICO give useful information specifically for dentists[11]. What, you didn't think you would get away with it that easily did you? A dental practice that provides NHS treatment (which means private practices are exempt) must adopt and maintain and publish the method by which "*specific information will be available so that it can be easily identified and accessed by members of the public*".

You are not obliged to inform the ICO that you have done this, but you must make a list of the information that is available.

You should explain how it can be accessed and the fee you will charge (fees are not allowed to be excessive and are usually frowned upon).

Appendix 4 contains a list of the information you are expected to have available

Access to Medical Reports Act 1988[12]

The **Access to Medical Reports Act** (AMRA) governs who has access to medical reports made by a health professional (includes dentists) for employment or insurance purposes only. Any other kind of report is covered by the DPA. Under the AMRA, patients retain the right to request access to a copy of the report up to 6 months following its supply to a third party.

A patient must give their consent before a report about them can be sent to an employer or insurer. A patient can apply for access to said report at any time before it is supplied to the third party. The dentist should not pass on the report to the third party until the report has been shown to the patient (unless they have specifically indicated they do not wish to see such information prior), unless 21 days have passed since the patient indicated that they wished to see the report.

Patient access to the report can be by either sending them a copy or allowing the patient to attend to view the report. Once seen, the dentists must wait until the patient gives their consent for the report to be passed on to the third party. The patient can ask to have the report amended if they believe it is incorrect. If you decline to amend, you need to attach a statement from the patient explaining why they feel the report is incorrect. Several further points to note:

- **All patient requests for amendments should be in writing.**
- **Patients ultimately have the right to refuse you permission to send the report.**
- **Dentists are not obliged to give access to any part of the report which may**
    - i. **Cause serious harm to the patient or others**
    - ii. **Indicate the intentions of the dentist towards the patient**
    - iii. **Identify a third person who has not consented to the information release, or who is not a health professional involved in the patient's care**

The Human Rights Act 1998[13]

There are some who think this no longer applies with the Brexit vote, but they are mistaken. The UK will still be signed up to the European Convention on Human Rights (ECHR) even when it leaves the EU (if you are reading this 10 year from now, it will be interesting to see how that all played out).

The UK courts have no option but to consider the Human Rights Act when dealing with confidentiality. Disclosure of patient information must comply with Article 8. However, this might only apply to NHS GDP's (who are contracted to a public authority, namely the NHS) and it is unlikely that you as a dentist will have to deal with this.

Article 8 - Right to respect for private and family life

1) **Everyone has the right to respect for his private and family life, his home and his correspondence.**
2) **There shall be no interference by a public authority with the exercise of this right except such as is in accordance with the law and is necessary in a**

democratic society in the interests of national security, public safety or the economic well-being of the country, for the prevention of disorder or crime, for the protection of health or morals, or for the protection of the rights and freedoms of others.

Specific to NHS

In the publication "**Confidentiality, the NHS Code of Practice**"[14] the following is written

A duty of confidence arises when one person discloses information to another (e.g. patient to clinician) in circumstances where it is reasonable to expect that information will be held in confidence. It -

a) Is a legal obligation that is derived from case law;
b) Is a requirement within professional codes of conduct;

Strangely it makes no mention of legislation. It does however go on to say that confidential information is information that can be used to identify patients. The code also states:

"The key principle of the duty of confidence is that information confided should not be used or disclosed further in an identifiable form, except as originally understood by the confider, or with his or her subsequent permission."

As someone who works under NHS contract, there are specific requirements that you need to meet under this NHS code of practice.

a) check where practicable that information leaflets on patient confidentiality and information disclosure have

been read and understood. These should be available within each NHS organisation; (you've got yours right?)

b) **make clear to patients when information is recorded or health records are accessed**; (Do your patients have this information?)

c) **make clear to patients when you will be disclosing information with others;**

d) **check that patients are aware of the choices available to them in respect of how their information may be disclosed and used;**

e) **check that patients have no concerns or queries about how their information is disclosed and used;**

f) **answer any queries personally or direct the patient to others who can answer their questions or other sources of information;**

g) **respect the rights of patients and help them in exercising their right to have access to their health records.**

You do not need a patient's permission to share their confidential information with certain organisations, because the patients give the NHS this right when they sign the FP17. By signing the FP17, the patient consents to their information being shared with the following organisations:

- **NHS Business Services Authority**
- **Other authorised bodies**

"Relevant" information can also be shared with

- **NHS England**
- **Department of Work and Pensions**
- **HM Revenue and Customs**
- **Local Authorities**

That is quite a substantial list when you think about it.

2006 NHS Dental Contract[15]

Remember the contract comes from a Statutory Instrument created by parliament. The contract has specific requirements that it places on Providers and Performers with regards confidentiality.

- The contractor must nominate a person responsible for the practice and procedures relating to the confidentiality of personal data
- You should provide any information requested by NHS England Local Area Teams (formally PCT's) to the NHS or to a person authorised by it in writing. This information includes the Contractor's patient records.

Records management - this will be dealt with in the Record keeping Section of this book

Confidentiality in adults who lack Capacity

Up until now we have been dealing with people who are able to make decisions about their own care. But there are people who do not have capacity to do this, and this topic is an absolute minefield. As I have said before (and will say numerous times throughout this book), in cases like this your best course of action in such instances is to seek the advice of your indemnifier (although how is the busy GDP to be assured an accurate response in a timely fashion?).

Let's see if we can shine any light on the topic. In her book Emily Jackson made the following observation:

"If the legal basis for the general duty of confidence is unclear, its application to children and adults who lack capacity is even more obscure." [16]

Why is this the case? As the DOH **Code of Practice on Protecting Confidentiality of Service User Information**[17] states:

The confidentiality requirement exists within a wider social context in which members of staff have other duties which may conflict with their duty of confidentiality…they may have other ethical duties to disclose confidential information, without consent, if serious dangers are present for third parties

In part 27 of Annex B **The NHS Code of Practice of Confidentiality:**[18]

The key principle of the duty of confidence is that information confided should not be used or disclosed further in an identifiable form, except as originally understood by the confider, or with his or her subsequent permission.

The challenge is that people who lack capacity cannot often understand what is being proposed, and aren't able to consent to information being shared. Thus medical clinicians need rules on how to deal with such situations, and it is preferable if this was in an easily understood format. You didn't think the bureaucrats were going to make it that easy did you?

One would think that the **Mental Capacity Act 2005**[19] would help with this, but really it doesn't. The Mental Capacity Act does mention disclosure in section 4, but it doesn't determine in which instances a clinician can discuss the non-capable adult's details. So we are left to refer to other guidance on the matter.

For example, in the guidance from the "**Office of the Public Guardian, *Making decisions, A guide for people who work in health and social care* (2009)**" the guidance states[20] that the situation is relatively straight forward where an Attorney under a Personal Welfare LPA has been appointed.

Where an Attorney under a Personal Welfare LPA has been appointed they will determine whether information can be disclosed and you must normally consult with them before sharing any information.

But such an appointment is not always available. Indeed, the difficulty for clinicians in this situation is also highlighted in the before mentioned guide

Disclosure of, and access to, information can be complex. The Information Commissioner has issued guidance on the Data Protection Act 1998, and the Mental Capacity Act does not change or substitute this. Also, professionals and organisations have their own codes of conduct, policies and procedures about confidentiality. These are supported by experts such as Information/Data Protection Officers in Social Services and Caldicott Guardians in NHS organisations.

To determine a lack of capacity an assessment must be done, and the explanatory note in the Mental Capacity Act (MCA) explains this further. The very act of defining capacity can in itself involve the sharing of confidential information. So how does the individual tasked with determining capacity move ahead when the patient declines consent for the sharing of that information? What if, in doing so, the patient is later deemed competent? Will the defence that the clinician was acting in the best interests of the patient be enough should the patient complain to the GDC? In its guidance **Confidentiality**[21] the General Medical Council (GMC) states:

If a patient who lacks capacity asks you not to disclose personal information about their condition or treatment, you should try to persuade them to allow an appropriate person to be involved in the consultation. If they refuse, and you are convinced that it is essential in their best interests, you may disclose relevant information to an appropriate person or authority.

One thing that is evident is the apparent contradiction between the GDC standards and the Mental Capacity Act. section.1(2) of the Mental Capacity Act states - ***A person must be assumed to have capacity unless it is established that he lacks capacity***. Whereas the GDC Standards For the Dental Team 3.2.4 states - ***You must always consider whether patients are able to make decisions about their care themselves, and avoid making assumptions about a patient's ability to give consent.*** I will let you form your own judgement on this issue.

Confidentiality and children

Some might think this is straightforward. Well, not so fast. In their book, Kennedy and Grubb make the following statement[22]

"In principle, the law is no different from that applicable to adults… A breach of confidence may be justified if, for example it is made in the public interest."

The **Children Act 1989**[23] and **Family Law Reform Act 1987**[24] (FLRA) both define a child as someone under 18, but the FLRA does allow for those over the age of 16 and 17 to consent to medical examination and treatment due to a rule in section 8 (Consent by persons over 16 to surgical, medical and dental treatment)

"(1) The consent of a minor who has attained the age of sixteen years to any surgical, medical or dental treatment which, in the absence of consent, would constitute a trespass to his person, shall be as effective as it would be if he were of full age"

The 2006 GDS contract also defines a child as "someone who has not attained the age of 16 years". So from the legislation, with certain exceptions, 16 and 17 year olds can be treated as adults with regards to consent. But is that the case with confidentiality?

"Confidentiality, the NHS Code of Practice" states that

"Young people aged 16 or 17 are presumed to be competent for the purposes of consent to treatment and are therefore entitled to the same duty of confidence as adults."

So for a child over 16 years of age, the guidance available states that they should be treated as an adult assuming there is no mental health competency issues, which would take us back to the challenges outlined previously. After all, under the NHS, anyone who reaches the age of 16 can sign their own FP17 form. This is not to stop you asking permission to discuss matters about a 16 year old's care with their parents. Remember though they are still classed as a child when it comes to safeguarding issues.

Next we will address the child under 16. Again from "Confidentiality, the NHS Code of Practice"

Children under 16 who have the capacity and understanding to take decisions about their own treatment are also entitled to decide whether personal information may be passed on and generally to have their confidence respected. The key issue here is the 'competence' of the child.... However, where a child has refused to consent to treatment for a life threatening condition, staff should inform parents and seek their consent

So here we have a specific instance mentioned where disclosure without consent can be made. The GMC have guidance which specifically relates to confidentiality:[25]

The same duties of confidentiality apply when using, sharing or disclosing information about children and young people as about adults.

The GMC guidance further states that competent children should be asked when the medical staff wish to share their confidential information. No mention is made of the parent in regards to the competent child, and it is assumed that the parent is one of the third parties to which confidential information can be shared. The guidance then goes on to state what is to be done if the competent child does not consent to the sharing of their confidential medical details:

If a child or young person refuses consent, or if it is not practical to ask for consent, you should consider the benefits and possible harms that may arise from disclosure. You should consider any views given by the child or young person on why you should not disclose the information. But you should disclose

information if this is necessary to protect the child or young person, or someone else, from risk of death or serious harm.

Because of the nature of what we do, there are many who argue that there will be very few instances where disclosure to a parent will not be justified. For example, I once had a fifteen-year-old turn up with a tongue piercing that was clearly infected. The Mother, whilst knowing about the piercing, had not consented to it and the child did not want me to impart the information that the tongue was clearly inflamed. It was a no brainer that the information needed to be shared because the wellbeing of the child was paramount. This subject will be further discussed in the consent section.

The Common law

Whilst what has been discussed shows how a dentist might be penalised should you break a patient's confidentiality, it doesn't show how the patient can be compensated. To do so they would need to take the matter up with a solicitor. Judges have generally agreed that there is a need for health practitioners to maintain their patient's confidentiality. The common law does therefore recognise that a legal obligation of confidence exists.

If you breach a patient's confidentiality, they may be able to sue you for the breach of that confidentiality. It would be difficult for them to do this through an action for negligence, because the breach alone (which would be argued as a breach of your duty of care) wouldn't be enough. They would have to show that damage ensued from the breach. Perhaps more likely then, the claim for damages will be made under breach of contract. Unfortunately for NHS patients this avenue is not open to them because there is no contractual relationship between patient and dentists if seen under the NHS.

In Summary

- Patient information should usually not be disclosed without the patient's permission.
- Only the minimum amount of information required should be released
- Rarely you may be justified in releasing confidential information without their permission, if for example a patient puts their own safety or the safety of others at risk. It may be prudent to release information if doing so can help prevent a serious crime. Your indemnifier will advise you on these occasions
- If a patient or their representative makes a request for records, determine under what legislation they are applying for the access. It may impact the fees you can charge and the types of information you can release.
- It is recommended that you do not post recognisable information about patients on social media.
- Any request for records made by another dentist in another practice must ideally be supported by a written authority from the patient.
- Get patients to fill out a "sharing of information" form which indicates who they allow you to share data and information with (see **Appendix 5**).
- You should have a way of identifying patients who contact the practice to determine their identity. Not everyone will be recognisable by voice, and even then set procedures should be followed.

- Reception areas must be free of visible patient information. If the computer screen can be seen by others, even if by someone leaning over reception, it is recommended to use a privacy screen. Also, workstations should be protected with a password protected screensaver if unattended. Hard copies of medical records must be kept in a locked cabinet (for example) when not being used. Remember, cleaning staff should not have access to said records.
- It is recommended that all staff (including non-clinical staff) sign a confidentiality agreement as part of their employment. This can be part of their contract of employment.
- Confidentiality applies to staff as well as patients. Personal details about staff should not be accessible by anyone other than those who need to deal with it (Practice Manager, practice owner, registered manager etc.).
- Testimonials and letters of gratitude must have specific patient consent before they can be displayed (patient lounge, website etc.) unless they can be thoroughly anonymised.
- With children, not all people who present will have parental responsibility. A dentist must be careful to only share information about a child with someone who has parental responsibility (see further in CONSENT)
- With regards disclosing in the public interest, the need for disclosure must be stronger than the public interest in maintaining the confidentiality.
- Have your indemnifier on speed-dial

Confidentiality References

1. **Confidentiality**: **Reporting gunshot and knife wounds** - General Medical Council, *Confidentiality: Reporting gunshot and knife wounds* (2009)
2. **Road Traffic Act 1988 -** https://www.legislation.gov.uk/ukpga/1988/52/contents
3. **Confidentiality -** https://www.dentalprotection.org/docs/librariesprovider4/dental-advice-booklets/dental-advice-booklet-confidentiality.pdf?sfvrsn=24
4. **GDC 2016:** Guidance on Using Social media - https://www.gdc-uk.org/api/files/Guidance%20on%20using%20social%20media.pdf
5. **Confidentiality: NHS Code of Practice** - https://digital.nhs.uk/article/1200/Confidentiality
6. **Guidance for Access to health Records Requests** - https://www.igt.hscic.gov.uk/WhatsNewDocuments/Access%20to%20Health%20Records%20Feb%202010.pdf
7. **Data Protection Act 1998 -** https://www.legislation.gov.uk/ukpga/1998/29/contents
8. **Data Protection Registration** - https://ico.org.uk/for-organisations/register/
9. **Access to Health Records Act 1990 -** https://www.legislation.gov.uk/ukpga/1990/23/contents
10. **Freedom of Information Act 2000 -** https://www.legislation.gov.uk/ukpga/2000/36/contents
11. **IOC Dentists guidance** - https://ico.org.uk/media/for-organisations/documents/1276/dentists_guidance.doc
12. **Access to Medical Reports Act 1988 -** https://www.legislation.gov.uk/ukpga/1988/28/contents
13. **The Human Rights Act 1998 -** https://www.legislation.gov.uk/ukpga/1998/42/contents

14. **Confidentiality, the NHS Code of Practice -** https://www.gov.uk/government/publications/confidentiality-nhs-code-of-practice
15. **2006 NHS Dental Contract -** http://www.legislation.gov.uk/uksi/2005/3361/pdfs/uksi_20053361_en.pdf
16. **Emily Jackson**, *Medical Law Text cases and materials* (3rd ed, Oxford University Press 2013) p.375
17. **DOH Code of Practice on Protecting Confidentiality of Service User Information -** Department of Health Social Services and Public Safety, *Code of Practice on Protecting Confidentiality of Service User Information,* (2012) p.54
18. **The NHS Code of Practice of Confidentiality -** Department of Health, *The NHS Code of Practice of Confidentiality* (2003)
19. **Mental Capacity Act 2005 -** https://www.legislation.gov.uk/ukpga/2005/9/contents
20. **Office of the Public Guardian, *Making decisions, A guide for people who work in health and social care* (2009)" -** http://www.ouh.nhs.uk/patient-guide/safeguarding/documents/health-workers-guide.pdf
21. **GMC: Confidentiality -** http://www.gmc-uk.org/Confidentiality_0513_Revised.pdf_52090934.pdf
22. **Kennedy and Grubb, *Medical Law***, (3rd ed. Butterworths 2000) p.1079
23. **Children Act 1989 -** https://www.legislation.gov.uk/ukpga/1989/41/contents
24. **Family Law Reform Act 1987 -** http://www.legislation.gov.uk/ukpga/1987/42
25. **GMC: 0-18 years -** http://www.gmc-uk.org/0_18_years___English_1015.pdf_48903188.pdf

Consent

Consent is too complex a topic to be covered in any depth in a publication such as this (whole books have been written on the subject). The purpose of this chapter will therefore be to give you an introduction to the subject of consent. Because of the complexity (many of the problematic consent situations you encounter will be unique and time consuming to deal with) we can only give a rough summary of the law and the guidance as it presently stands.

In my opinion, this is the most important topic because the implications of failing to obtain consent can be severe. This is the definition of consent from the 1983 Mental Health Act Code of Practice[1]

"Consent is the voluntary and continuing permission of a patient to be given a particular treatment, based on a sufficient knowledge of the purpose, nature, likely effects and risks of that treatment, including the likelihood of its success and any alternatives to it"

The duty of care owed by a dentist to his/her patient includes the duty to obtain consent, and a failure to obtain consent could be seen as a breach of that duty and thus would fall into the realms of negligence (if you are lucky). Consent is important because it allows the patient to fully understand what you are doing (the days of dental paternalism are now long gone) and if consent is attained, it also protects the dentist in medico legal matters, specifically the charge of battery which can be career ending.

The rules on consent come from various arenas. There is common law, instructions by your regulator as well as actual legislation. I will list a few here to give you an overall picture, and some of these will be covered shortly in more detail. Much of the law dealing with consent in a competent adult has been formulated by judges through various court cases (the available legislation deals primarily with consent for those who lack the capacity to give that consent themselves).

- **GDC Standards Principle 3**
- **Family Law Reform Act 1969**
- **Mental Capacity Act 2005**
- **Mental health Act Code of Practice 2007**
- **Common law e.g. Sidaway v Bethlem Royal Hospital Governors, and Montgomery v Lanarkshire Health board**

A situation that sometimes arises is a patient who sits before you and says "I don't want to know anything". Can you be sure they actually mean this and what do you do? In this situation it is best to discuss the matter with your indemnifier. You might not have encountered this scenario before, but I guarantee you they will have.

Battery or Negligence?

If treatment goes wrong (when there is a lack of consent) and the patient sues, which avenue are they likely to go for? Pre Montgomery, it was harder to prove the tort of trespass (against the person, aka battery) than it was to prove negligence via lack of consent. To quote Judge Bristow in the 1981 case **Chatterton v Gerson:**[2]

"once a patient is informed in broad terms of the nature of the procedure which is intended, and gives her consent, that consent is real, and the cause of the action on which to base a claim for

failure to go into risks and implications is negligence, not trespass"

Prior to the Montgomery ruling there was another case in 2015 called **Border V Lewisham and Greenwich NHS Trust**[3]. In essence the doctor involved wanted to put an IV line in the 64-year-old patient's arm even though there was no urgent need for it. Only one arm was available due to the other arm being injured. Unfortunately, the patient had a susceptibility to oedema which subsequently occurred. The patient sued and eventually won (on appeal) on negligence because the doctor did it against her express consent. At the appeal hearing the patient raised a matter not brought up at the initial trial, that by not getting her consent, the doctor was guilty of the tort of trespass. The court of appeal found the doctor guilty of negligence, breach of duty being found through failure to obtain consent. They rejected the attempt to add a claim in the tort of trespass. You are probably thinking the medical profession (and thus us) dodged a bullet there.

Looking through recent cases there does not as yet appear to be a rush to bring claims through the tort of trespass. This may be due to a reluctance on the part of Judges to go down this road. To quote Judge Bristow from Chatterton v Gerson again:

"it would be very much against the interests of justice if actions which were really based on a failure by the doctor to perform his duty adequately to inform were pleaded in trespass."

This is not to say that where a lack of consent exists, a patient cannot attempt to bring a case under the tort of trespass. In fact, if no consent exists then it could be argued that the case SHOULD be brought under trespass. So think about the treatment you do. You are replacing an MOD on the UR5 and you find a small M cavity on the UR6. Do you just fill it, or sit the patient up and get their express consent? As small a lesion as it might seem to you, it might be a big deal to the patient. Some form of consent for the extra restoration needs to be acquired. So, here are some scenarios you as a dentist need to avoid:

- Doing treatment on a patient without their knowledge or consent. The question of how much information the patient needs will come out in your co-diagnosis conversation with them
- Do not treat the competent patient under duress or against their will. I remember seeing a lecture about an American emergency clinic, where the clinician then put up a picture with the comment "and this is our restraint board." If you remember the old "restraint" question the CQC posed you, I'm sure you remember that the easiest and best answer would be "we never restrain patients".
- Do not persuade patients to have treatment by giving them the wrong information. This does produce a dilemma for NHS practitioners because just what exactly is and isn't available under the NHS? Misleading information such as "implants last forever" are also to be avoided.
- Don't say you are going to do treatment X and then do treatment Y. For example, don't say you are going to do an amalgam and then put in a composite without the patient's express permission.

Remember, a case brought under the tort of trespass does not have the same threshold for the defendant as one brought under negligence. We will discuss Montgomery at greater length in the **NEGLIGENCE** section later on.

Implied consent

If a competent patient sits in your dental chair, allows you to sit them back and opens their mouth, it can be implied that they have given their consent for you to examine them. Even so, I would personally advise explicitly asking them. For example, if you wished to examine the Muscles of Mastication on a new patient, it would be wise to first advise them the reasons why you were doing this and seek their permission before doing so. It is not beyond the realms of possibility that they have never had this done before. Not all dentists are as ethical and as thorough as you.

Express consent

Getting consent in compliance with Montgomery is the same process of getting valid express consent. You examine, acquire information and then give information to elicit the treatment plan that is right for the patient. Dentistry is no longer the place for fancy sales techniques (in fact it never was) and you are not here to sell treatments but to build rapport and create a professional relationship built on trust. Whilst you are able to give your clinical opinion on what YOU think is best for the patient, it's important to remember that ten dentists will come up with ten different treatment plans for the same mouth. Your opinion is not THE opinion. This is why the GDC say you should give all the valid options with the risks and benefits.

To get consent you also need to gather information about the patient. This is part of the rapport building process, where you exchange thoughts and ideas so as to build up a picture of what the patient wants from you. Consent is NOT putting a 36-page manual with "risk of death" at the end of a long list of risks for every procedure. That is the American way, and it does not work in the UK because our laws are different. In America you can sign your rights away. This is not the case in the UK.

Consent must be tailored to the individual and thus takes time. It cannot be done in a 5-minute check-up. And whilst it can be done by trained dental nurses (for example) the clinician doing the treatment is ultimately responsible for the gaining of that consent. It won't be the dental nurse that gets sued.

I call this process co-diagnosis, working with the patient to find out their wants and needs. By doing so you uphold the autonomy of the patient, respecting their right to control what is done to their body. And as is sometimes the case, you may not agree with the patient's decision. You might feel you can, for example save the tooth, but they might decide extraction is best for them. Whilst you should not feel forced to do treatment that you feel is not in the patient's best interests, you should also respect their wishes. At the end of the day, patients have the right to make "foolish decisions" about their own health, just so long as they have the correct level of information to make those decisions.

The respect for a competent person to have autonomy over their own body is enshrined in English Common law (we will discuss those who lack capacity shortly). This is why a competent Jehovah's Witness can refuse a blood transfusion and not have such a transfusion forced upon them, even if the transfusion is the only thing that will save their life. This is why you have to be very careful in your consent, as some people will need to know every detail of what you are putting in their mouths.

Some common things that might trip you up (they might seem minor to us, but to some patients they are extremely important):

- Some patients might not know that amalgam contains mercury and may object to it being placed
- Some anti-fluoride advocates will not want any fluoride releasing restoration placed in their mouths
- Some materials may have religious implications based on where the materials are derived from

And yes, this does make the consent process particularly problematic. It is our job as professionals to weave our way through the legal minefield and get to the other side...a healthy mouth, well restored and disease free in a happy patient.

Common law

Before Montgomery there was Sidaway. Sidaway was a case about the information given to a patient prior to spinal surgery. The surgeon failed to warn about the condition that subsequently occurred and the patient sued on the argument that if she had been warned she likely would not have gone ahead with the procedure. The court took expert witness evidence and agreed with the Bolam defence that a reasonable body of opinion would not have warned about the risk and so it was not negligent. This was replaced by the Montgomery ruling.

Human Rights Act (HRA)

One point of interest to those providing care under NHS contract. NHS organisations are public bodies, and thus have to comply with the HRA. This will apply to subcontractors too, so there is a possibility that failure to obtain valid consent would not only risk an accusation of battery but also an accusation that you had breached that patient's human rights, especially if the treatment went wrong and caused pain and/or discomfort. If you want to be specific we are dealing with Article 3 of the act

"No one shall be subjected to torture or to inhuman or degrading treatment or punishment"

Technically a Private practice that receives no form of government funding (at all) would be exempt from having to comply with the act. Only the courts have the power to decide on this kind of thing, but it does open up another avenue for litigious patients to pursue. Can you see how the law makes it easier to practice privately compared to under NHS contract.

The GDC

Once again the GDC set aside a whole principle to this issue.

3. Obtain Valid Consent

3.1 You must obtain valid consent before starting treatment, explaining all the relevant options and the possible costs
Guidance - Comment: If you are the treating clinician, YOU have to ensure that YOU get consent from the patient. By all means use treatment coordinators, but it's your responsibility at the end of the day. Never forget that.

3.1.1 You must make sure you have valid consent before starting any treatment or investigation. This applies whether you are the first member of your team to see the patient or whether you are involved after other team members have already seen them. Do not assume that someone else has obtained the patient's consent.

- **Comment**: You must give the patient all the viable options, with the pros and cons and record this discussion in the notes.

3.1.2 You <u>should</u> document the discussions you have with patients in the process of gaining consent. Although a signature on a form is important in verifying that a patient has given consent, it is the discussions that take place with the patient that determine whether the consent is valid. - **Comment**: A signed consent form does not indicate the patient understands what they have signed. It is in fact fairly useless in UK law.

3.1.3 You <u>should</u> find out what your patients want to know as well as what you think they need to know. Things that patients might want to know include:

- ***options for treatment, their risks and potential benefits;***
- ***why you think a particular treatment is necessary and appropriate for them;***
- ***the consequences, risks and benefits of the treatment you propose;***
- ***the likely prognosis;***
- ***your recommended option;***
- ***the cost of proposed treatment;***
- ***what might happen if the proposed treatment is not carried out; and***
- ***whether the treatment is guaranteed, how long it is guaranteed for and any exclusions that apply.***

- **Comment**: This is where common law (through Montgomery) has caught up with the regulator. Remember you need to determine the information the patient needs to give their consent.

3.1.4 You <u>must</u> check and document that patients have understood the information you have given. - **Comment**: You must check and write down that the patient has understood the information

3.1.5 Patients can withdraw their consent at any time, refuse treatment or ask for it to be stopped after it has started. You must acknowledge their right to do this and follow their wishes. You should explain the consequences or risks of not continuing the treatment and ensure that the patient knows that they are responsible for any future problems which arise as a result of not completing the treatment. You must record all this in the patient's notes.

3.1.6 You must obtain written consent where treatment involves conscious sedation or general anaesthetic. - **Comment**: Even though written consent doesn't prove anything; you must obtain written consent for tx involving GA or Conscious sedation. Perhaps it's just me, but I was never able to find an official template for consent for RA.

3.2 You must make sure that patients (or their representatives) understand the decisions they are being asked to make

3.2.1 You must provide patients with sufficient information and give them a reasonable amount of time to consider that information in order to make a decision. - **Comment**: Notice that the GDC does not define what they consider reasonable. They also offer no guidance on what information you should give. How then can you be fully confident you have met this standard? Is it perhaps completely open to interpretation? Does this also mean you cannot fix a broken tooth on the same appointment where the patient presents with their complaint? This is one of the issues with regulation. No matter how it is written, there will be questions about its interpretation.

3.2.2 You must tailor the way you obtain consent to each patient's needs. You should help them to make informed decisions about their care by giving them information in a format they can easily understand. - **Comment**: In my opinion (and that's all it is, an opinion) this is an impossible standard to meet 100% of the time. A patient can say "yes I understand all that" just so as not to appear unintelligent in your eyes. Remember, one of the biggest fears patients have is that of feeling humiliated. Again there is no guidance on how to meet this standard from the GDC itself. Should someone then make a complaint, it could be argued that all they have to do is state "I did not understand the tx proposed". Defendable, but a challenge. I know of one well renowned implant dentist who makes his patients pass a test to show that they have read and understood his treatment plan.

3.2.3 When obtaining consent, you <u>should</u> encourage patients who have communication difficulties to have a friend, relative or carer with them to help them ask questions or understand your answers.

3.2.4 You <u>must</u> always consider whether patients are able to make decisions about their care themselves, and avoid making assumptions about a patient's ability to give consent. This is a complex area and you should refer to the appropriate legislation. You can find further information on our website or you can contact your defence organisation for further advice. -
<u>Comment</u>: I have a big problem with this standard. It states you must

avoid making assumptions about a patient's ability to give consent. This potentially contradicts Section 1(2) of the Mental Capacity Act 2005, and I quote – "A person must be assumed to have capacity (to give consent) unless it is established the he lacks capacity". The GDC disagree on my interpretation on this when I wrote to them about it.

3.2.5 You <u>must</u> check and document that patients have understood the information you have given them.

3.3 You must make sure that the patient's consent remains valid at each stage of investigation or treatment

3.3.1 Giving and obtaining consent is a process, not a one-off event. It should be part of on-going communication between patients and all members of the dental team involved in their care. You should keep patients informed about the progress of their care.

3.3.2 When carrying out an on-going course of treatment, you must make sure you have specific consent for what you are going to do during that appointment. **Comment** - do you ask every patient if they understand what you plan to do to them at every appointment?

3.3.3 You must tailor the way you confirm ongoing consent to each patient's needs and check that patients have understood the information you have given them.

3.3.4 You must document the discussions you have with patients in the process of confirming their ongoing consent. - **Comment**: Remember, it says ongoing consent. So not only do you need to check that the patient understands what you are doing, you need to record that discussion. If you aren't already doing this, don't worry, you will still have time to do the dentistry, you just need to adjust your way of working slightly.

3.3.5 If you think that you need to change a patient's agreed treatment or the estimated cost, you must obtain your patient's consent to the changes and document that you have done so.

Failure to gain consent would be looked upon unfavourably by the GDC.

The CQC

Your other regulator also has very strict rules on consent Which is covered by their Regulation 11[4]:

- ***Care and treatment of service users must only be provided with the consent of the relevant person.***
- ***Paragraph (1) is subject to paragraphs (3) and (4).***
- ***If the service user is 16 or over and is unable to give such consent because they lack capacity to do so, the registered person must act in accordance with the 2005 MCA***
- **But if Part 4 or 4A of the 1983 Mental health Act applies to a service user, the registered person must act in accordance with the provisions of that Act.**
- **Nothing in this regulation affects the operation of section 5 of the 2005 Mental Capacity Act, as read with section 6 of that Act (acts in connection with care or treatment).**

Their further guidance goes on to advise:

- ***When a person is asked for their consent, information about the proposed care and treatment must be provided in a way that they can understand. This should include information about the risks, complications and any alternatives. A person with the necessary knowledge and understanding of the care and treatment should provide this information so that they can answer any questions about it to help the person consent to it.***
- ***Discussions about consent must be held in a way that meets people's communication needs. This may include the use of different formats or languages and may involve others such as a speech language therapist or independent advocate. Consent may be implied and include non-verbal***

communication such as sign language or by someone rolling up their sleeve to have their blood pressure taken or offering their hand when asked if they would like help to move.

- *Consent must be treated as a process that continues throughout the duration of care and treatment, recognising that it may be withheld and/or withdrawn at any time.*
- *When a person using a service or a person acting lawfully on their behalf refuses to give consent or withdraws it, all people providing care and treatment must respect this.*
- *Where a person lacks mental capacity to make an informed decision, or give consent, staff must act in accordance with the requirements of the Mental Capacity Act 2005 and associated code of practice.*
- *Consent procedures must make sure that people are not pressured into giving consent and, where possible, plans must be made well in advance to allow time to respond to people's questions and provide adequate information.*
- *Policies and procedures for obtaining consent to care and treatment must reflect current legislation and guidance, and staff must follow them at all times.*
- *Providers must make sure that staff who obtain the consent of people who use the service are familiar with the principles and codes of conduct associated with the Mental Capacity Act 2005, and are able to apply those when appropriate, for any of the people they are caring for.*

Children & Young Adults

We have already discussed the definitions of children and young adults. As a reminder, when it comes to dental consent, the term children includes anyone below the age of 16. Young adults are anyone aged 16 and 17.

With regards children's consent there are two main parties:

- The people with parental responsibility
- The child/young adult themselves

Now most people, when they think "parental responsibility" will think Mum and Dad, but it's not as clear cut as that. The definition of Parental responsibility is actually set out in legislation which defines exactly who has the authority to give consent for a child's treatment. And of course there is also the issue of declining consent.

The meaning of parental responsibility is shown by section 3 of the **Children Act 1989**[5].

3 Meaning of "parental responsibility".

(1) In this Act "parental responsibility" means all the rights, duties, powers, responsibilities and authority which by law a parent of a child has in relation to the child and his property.

(2) It also includes the rights, powers and duties which a guardian of the child's estate (appointed, before the commencement of section 5, to act generally) would have had in relation to the child and his property.

(3) The rights referred to in subsection (2) include, in particular, the right of the guardian to receive or recover in his own name, for the benefit of the child, property of whatever description and wherever situated which the child is entitled to receive or recover.

(4) The fact that a person has, or does not have, parental responsibility for a child shall not affect—

(a)any obligation which he may have in relation to the child (such as a statutory duty to maintain the child); or

(b)any rights which, in the event of the child's death, he (or any other person) may have in relation to the child's property.

(5)A person who—

(a)does not have parental responsibility for a particular child; but

(b)has care of the child, may (subject to the provisions of this Act) do what is reasonable in all the circumstances of the case for the purpose of safeguarding or promoting the child's welfare.

The British Medical Association produced guidance to aid the medical professional through the process of consent when it comes to parental responsibility[6]. This guidance outlines the position of parental responsibility.

1. ***"Parental responsibility refers to the rights, duties, powers and responsibilities that most parents have in respect of their children.***
2. ***Parental responsibility includes the right of parents to consent to treatment on behalf of their children, provided the treatment is in the interests of the child.***
3. ***Competent children can decide many aspects of their care for themselves.***
4. ***Where doctors believe that parental decisions are not in the best interests of the child, it may be necessary to seek a view from the courts, whilst meanwhile only providing emergency treatment that is essential to preserve life or prevent serious deterioration."***

The BMA guidance goes on to further say

"Parental responsibility is a legal concept that consists of the rights, duties, powers, responsibilities and authority that most parents have in respect of their children. It includes the right to give consent to medical treatment, although as is discussed below, this right is not absolute, as well as, in certain circumstances, the freedom to delegate some decision-making responsibility to others."

So who exactly has parental responsibility? Well, again that is defined by the **1989 Children Act**. Now get ready for this, because it's a bit long winded:

2 Parental responsibility for children.

(1) Where a child's father and mother were married to each other at the time of his birth, they shall each have parental responsibility for the child.

(1A) Where a child—

(a)has a parent by virtue of section 42 of the Human Fertilisation and Embryology Act 2008; or

(b)has a parent by virtue of section 43 of that Act and is a person to whom section 1(3) of the Family Law Reform Act 1987 applies, the child's mother and the other parent shall each have parental responsibility for the child.

(2) Where a child's father and mother were not married to each other at the time of his birth—

(a)the mother shall have parental responsibility for the child;

(b)the father shall have parental responsibility for the child if he has acquired it (and has not ceased to have it)] in accordance with the provisions of this Act.

(2A) Where a child has a parent by virtue of section 43 of the Human Fertilisation and Embryology Act 2008 and is not a person to whom section 1(3) of the Family Law Reform Act 1987 applies—

(a)the mother shall have parental responsibility for the child;

(b)the other parent shall have parental responsibility for the child if she has acquired it (and has not ceased to have it) in accordance with the provisions of this Act.]

(3) References in this Act to a child whose father and mother were, or (as the case may be) were not, married to each other at the time of his birth must be read with section 1 of the M1Family Law Reform Act 1987 (which extends their meaning).

(4) The rule of law that a father is the natural guardian of his legitimate child is abolished.

(5) More than one person may have parental responsibility for the same child at the same time.

(6) A person who has parental responsibility for a child at any time shall not cease to have that responsibility solely because some other person subsequently acquires parental responsibility for the child.

(7) Where more than one person has parental responsibility for a child, each of them may act alone and without the other (or others) in meeting that responsibility; but nothing in this Part shall be taken to affect the operation of any enactment which requires the consent of more than one person in a matter affecting the child.

(8)The fact that a person has parental responsibility for a child shall not entitle him to act in any way which would be incompatible with any order made with respect to the child under this Act.

(9)A person who has parental responsibility for a child may not surrender or transfer any part of that responsibility to another but may arrange for some or all of it to be met by one or more persons acting on his behalf.

(10)The person with whom any such arrangement is made may himself be a person who already has parental responsibility for the child concerned.
(11)The making of any such arrangement shall not affect any liability of the person making it which may arise from any failure to meet any part of his parental responsibility for the child concerned.

There you go, as clear as mud. Why don't you go and make yourself a cup of tea so you can recover from that? Oh, you've already opened the wine, well played. Don't worry, I'm going to summarise it for you:

- **All mothers have automatic parental responsibility**
- **Fathers have parental responsibility if they are named on the birth certificate and the child's birth was registered from 1st December 2003**
- **A Father will have PR if he was married to the mother at the time of the birth**
- **Other individuals can gain parental responsibility via a court order**
- **If both parents have parental responsibility, only one needs to give their permission**

So what do you do when the 14-year-old with toothache is brought in by the neighbour? Reading all that, can you think of any other scenarios you might face in your practice when it comes to getting someone with parental responsibility to consent to treatment? Here are a few:

1. Gillick competence

Did you know you are all child psychologists? A flippant comment I know, and it reflects that we, as dentists, are supposed to be able to determine the mental maturity of the children who come to see us.

Gillick refers to the 1985 case ***Gillick v West Norfolk and Wisbech Area Health Authority***[7]. It is arguably the most important case reflecting the rights of children under sixteen to consent to medical treatment. In deliberation, Lord Fraser stated parental rights were there solely to benefit the child. This case helped give competent under 16's the right to consent to certain medical treatments, thus limiting parental powers in this matter. So for a parent to override a Gillick competent child consenting to medical treatment that is in their best interests, the opinion of S.Wooley[8] becomes relevant:

> ***"In a child under 16, four main issues arise: (1) the child's capacity to consent to treatment; (2) parental authority and its limitations; (3) whose view prevails when parents and children clash; and (4) the extent of the courts' powers over adolescents. Gillick v West Norfolk considered the first three issues…. If they*** **(children)** ***failed this competency test, parental consent is required. Unfortunately, treatment refusal was not considered."***

Would you, as a dentist, want to go against parental wishes however? Also remember that Gillick does not give the competent child the right to refuse treatment. Gillick is a useful ruling where a competent child turns up needing treatment in the absence of someone with parental responsibility. If the child agrees to the treatment that is required in their best interests, the courts say you are allowed to go ahead with it.

However, are you absolutely certain the child has fully understood the need for what is required? What if there is a choice for their treatment? What if there are private options? Personally I would be happy to go ahead with basic treatment, but stuff like extractions and large restorations would be best done after the parents input (make sure to seek the approval of the Gillick competent child re: confidentiality first). Whilst it will be rare for a child to not want their parents involved in their dental care, it can happen so do not be afraid to seek advice on the matter. Also, one might consider developing an information leaflet that can be given to parents which explains the importance of consent etc.

I once had a child who was happy to have the treatment done (an amalgam) but the presenting parent was adamant that it should not be. "I don't want that poison in my boy's mouth" came the resounding battle cry. I dealt with that by education and compromise, which is sometimes all you have left in your arsenal. The child left with the all too familiar "*Mum, you're always causing a fuss*".

2. What if the parents don't agree to a Non Gillick competent child's treatment?

This is the sort of scenario you need to phone your indemnifier about. I know I say that a lot, and as I am sure you have guessed, there is a very good reason for this. A book like this cannot give proper advice for individual scenarios which will have a host of issues unknown to the writer. And as most of our treatments need to be done on conscious and cooperative patients, this adds further challenges.

From a medical point of view, medical professionals can ask the court's opinion when those with parental responsibility disagree with the proposed care of the child. The case of **Re A (Minors) (Conjoined Twins: Separation)**[9] was one such example. This litigation regarded the conjoined twin's M and J.

This was an appeal by the parents (who disagreed on religious grounds) of a previous judgment with medical opinion that surgical separation of the conjoined twins was needed to save J at the expense of the life of M, and that without such intervention both twins would die. The parents appealed on the basis that the original judge was in error in his conclusions, but the appeal was dismissed. It was considered that the sacrifice of M was needed to save J, and that if M had been born as a separate baby, it would not have survived.

In this case the religious wishes of the parents went against best medical opinion, and the parents were overruled and the operation was permitted. Although parents have rights regarding the welfare of their children, Lord Justice Robert Walker laid out the courts position:

"Therefore the court is bound by the overriding welfare principle in s.1(1) of that Act: "the child's welfare shall be the court's paramount consideration.""

The act referred to by Lord Justice Walker was of course the Children Act 1989 section 1(1)

(1)When a court determines any question with respect to—
(a)the upbringing of a child; or
(b)the administration of a child's property or the application of any income arising from it,
the child's welfare shall be the court's paramount consideration.

Lord Ward, whilst respecting the parent's decision nevertheless stated

"There is, however, this important safeguard to ensure that a child receives proper treatment. Because the parental rights and

powers exist for the performance of their duties and responsibilities to the child and must be exercised in the best interests of the child, "...the common law has never treated such rights as sovereign or beyond review and control", (see Gillick v West Norfolk and Wisbech Area Health Authority [1985] 3 All ER 402 at 420, [1986] 1 AC 112 at 184 per Lord Scarman.)"

Lord Ward explained the courts position thusly

"Long, long ago the sovereign's prerogative to protect infants passed to the Lord Chancellor and through him to the judges and it forms a part of the inherent jurisdiction of the High Court. The Children Act 1989 now contains a statutory scheme for the resolution of disputes affecting the upbringing of children. If a person having a recognisable interest brings such a dispute to the court, the court must decide it."

In the case of Re A (Minors), there was found to be justification for this decision in previous case law, in the 1993 case **Airedale NHS Trust v Bland**[10]. This involved a 17-year-old victim of the Hillsborough disaster who was deemed to be in a Persistent Vegetative State. The available body of medical opinion stated that the patient should be allowed to die, something the father agreed to. The declaration was granted, and this was held on an appeal made by the Official Solicitor. Although this is not a case of medical opinion going against both parental wishes, it reinforces the role of the courts in cases involving children where there is a difference of opinion in those with parental responsibility. Sir Thomas Bingham M.R. outlined the purpose of the courts in such cases:

"In cases where assessment of the patient's best interests is not undertaken by the court itself (as in wardship), the doctors' assessment is nonetheless subject to the courts review, where its jurisdiction is invoked"

There have been other cases that have seen the wishes of the parents overruled by the courts for what was seen to be the welfare of the child. In Re C[11] doctors wanted to do a HIV test on the child because the mother herself was HIV positive, but the parents refused. On appeal, the courts ordered the test to be done against the parents' wishes. Judge Wilson stated:

"It is accepted on all sides that the parents' wishes are of great importance; but it is still worthwhile to reflect how they interlock with the overarching inquiry into the baby's welfare…….But this case is not at its heart about the rights of the parents…….This baby has rights of her own"

Such cases will be few and far between in dentistry. The common things you will encounter are parent's refusal for the child to have amalgam or fluoride, both issues very big in the minds of some parents. Often the best course of action is to "advise, refer, leave and review". Referral to secondary care for a second, more authoritative opinion can often tip the balance in the parents agreeing to have the treatment done. Also be mindful that refusal to consent to treatment where there is active disease and a failure to change dietary and oral health patterns….well this could be viewed by some as a safeguarding issue. Always seek advice. Use your indemnifier, you pay a lot for it, and they will not penalise you (they bloody better not) for asking advice on such issues.

3. What if the parent says no, but the young adult says yes?

If both parent and young adult agree that treatment should be done, then really there is no issue so long as the treatment is being done in the young adult's best interests. Except in cases of deep psychological need, many cosmetic procedures, for example, are best left until full adulthood. Whilst parents are deemed to have rights with regards the upbringing of their children, when it comes to medical matters, the legislatory process and the courts have determined that the young adult also has rights, some of which cannot be overridden by said parents. Young Adults can consent to medical examination and treatment (with certain indicated exceptions) due to a rule in section 8 (Consent by persons over 16 to surgical, medical and dental treatment) of the Family Law Reform Act 1969.

> ***"The consent of a minor who has attained the age of sixteen years to any surgical, medical or dental treatment which, in the absence of consent, would constitute a trespass to his person, shall be as effective as it would be if he were of full age; and where a minor has by virtue of this section given an effective consent to any treatment it shall not be necessary to obtain any consent for it from his parent or guardian"***

Those with parental responsibility cannot usually override a competent young adult consenting to treatment that the dentist determines is in their best interests. Remember though that the law in this regard is complex and if necessary, advice should be sought. It is always better to have all the parties involved on board.

4. What if the young adult says no?

With regards young adults, the parents have far less say regarding the decisions of their care. Whilst it is advisable for you to ask the young adult to include their parents in decisions, they are deemed to have the rights of adults and if there is a question of competency, this will be the same test faced by adults. Young adults can be presumed to have capacity to consent or decline consent for their own treatment. Competent young adults have the right to decline treatment, although their parents may be able to persuade them otherwise. There will be very few occasions in dentistry where you would need to go to the Court of Protection to overrule a Young adult.

The Mental Capacity Act does provide two exceptions however, in that 16 and 17 year olds "*cannot make a Lasting Power of Attorney*" or an "*advanced decision on future care.*" However, for those children over 16 who lack capacity, then parental consent can be sought, or the courts can be asked to provide consent, as outlined in the official Department of Health guidance "**Seeking Consent: Working with Children**"[12]

5. What if the parent says yes but the child says no?

Remember a Gillick competent child has no right to refuse treatment. It will be down to you and the parents to persuade them to have the treatment done, but I'm sure you are all aware of the difficulties in treating an uncooperative child. You may have to delay treatment, or even refer to secondary care.

The non-competent adult

Not all adults have the capacity to understand and comprehend the treatment you propose. Dementia and certain mental health conditions can cause problems with a patient's understanding and retention of information, and such patients will often attend your practice with carers or relatives. Who can you discuss consent with?

The Mental Capacity Act 2005 covers the treatment of adults who lack capacity. The act sets out the five keys (section 1 of the act) regarding consent

1)You should assume a patient has capacity unless proven otherwise

2) You should take every possible measure to help those without capacity to understand the procedure. People should be supported to make their own decisions.

3) Making what a dentist classes as an "unwise decision" does not indicate a lack of capacity

4) Any treatment or decision made for someone who lacks capacity must be in their best interests

5) If you do try to treat a patient who lacks capacity, your actions should be the most respectful option with regards their rights and freedoms

Assessing capacity:

The Mental Capacity Act determines a lack of capacity as

"someone who is unable to make a decision for themselves in relation to the matter because of an impairment of, or a

***disturbance in the functioning of the mind or brain….it does not matter if the impairment or disturbance is permanent or temporary*"**

Your decision on assessing capacity is based on what you determine to be the balance of probability. Sometimes such conditions are obvious, sometimes not so. Do you as a dentist have the psychological knowledge to be able to assess a patient properly? The elderly gentleman who keeps turning up day after day for an appointment he has already had is clearly someone who may lack capacity. But what about a younger person who has no history, but starts acting irrationally?

When assessing capacity, you must consider two things:

1) **Does the patient present with an impairment of the mind/brain that affects the way their mind/brain works?**
2) **Does the impairment or disturbance stop the patient making decisions at the specific instance those decisions need to be made (remember, incapacity may be temporary)?**

As the Mental Capacity Act states in section 3:

"3. Inability to make decisions

(1) For the purposes of section 2, a person is unable to make a decision for himself if he is unable—

(a)to understand the information relevant to the decision,
(b)to retain that information,

(c)to use or weigh that information as part of the process of making the decision, or

(d)to communicate his decision (whether by talking, using sign language or any other means).

(2) A person is not to be regarded as unable to understand the information relevant to a decision if he is able to understand an explanation of it given to him in a way that is appropriate to his circumstances (using simple language, visual aids or any other means).

(3) The fact that a person is able to retain the information relevant to a decision for a short period only does not prevent him from being regarded as able to make the decision."

Assessing what is in the patient's best interests:

The BMA give very good guidance on this[13]

"When determining what is in the patient's best interests, a number of factors should be addressed including:

- *the patient's own wishes and values (where these can be ascertained), including any advance decision*
- *clinical judgement about the effectiveness of the proposed treatment, particularly in relation to other options*
- *where there is more than one option, which option is less restrictive of the patient's future choices*
- *the likelihood and extent of any degree of improvement in the patient's condition if treatment is provided*
- *the views of the parents, if the patient is a child*
- *the views of people close to the patient, especially close relatives, partners, carers, welfare attorneys, court-appointed deputies or guardians*
- *about what the patient is likely to see as beneficial; and*

- ***any knowledge of the patient's religious, cultural and other non-medical views that might have an impact on the patient's wishes."***

We are perhaps lucky, as dentists, that we rarely have to deal with life threatening conditions. But we do have to deal with situations that can result in pain and considerable discomfort either by our intervention or the lack of such.

So with regards to treatment who do we consult? We have to be mindful about the rights to confidentiality whilst taking actions that are in the patient's best interests. Dental Protection Limited offer the following advice (in their document **Consent**[14]) on who to contact:

- **"If it is practical and appropriate to do so, consult other people for their views about the person's best interests and to see if they have any information about the person's wishes and feelings, beliefs and values. In particular, try to consult:**
    - **Anyone previously named by the person as someone to be consulted on either the decision in question or on similar issues. (remember the sharing information form in the appendix?)**
    - **Anyone engaged in caring for the person**
    - **Close relatives, friends or others who take an interest in the person's welfare.**
    - **Any attorney appointed under a Lasting Power of Attorney or Enduring Power of Attorney made by the person.**
    - **Any deputy appointed by the Court of Protection to make decisions for the person.**

- **For decisions about major medical treatment, where no-one fits into any of the above categories an Independent Mental Capacity advocate (IMCA) must be consulted."**

Overruling consent and Patients who refuse treatment

In general dental practice there will be virtually no occasions when you would want to overrule the consent of a competent individual. When it comes to competent adults who refuse treatment that you think is in their best interests, it has to be said again that, in English law, people are allowed to make "foolish decisions" about their own health. My use of the word foolish is more to reflect how some clinicians view such patients rather than the actual decision being made by them. For the majority, dentistry is unpleasant, and the desire to avoid unpleasant experiences is understandable, even if that means facing a worse experience later on. We are not psychologists, we are dentists.

The competent adult may refuse treatment, even if that results in their death or physical harm, and only a court of law can override that decision, which they are often loath to do. There are very few occasions in general dentistry where you would want to seek the court's help to make a patient undergo treatment. In fact, I can't actually think of any so really this isn't an area that concerns us.

The other problem is that, even if the courts did decide the treatment needed doing, how on earth would you do it? The patient would never attend, and even if they did, they wouldn't lie there and let you fettle about in their mouths. The issue with refusal relates to children and those without capacity.

When consent isn't needed

There are limited incidences when you do not require a patient's consent. These are mainly based around medical emergencies where the patient is incapacitated. Also in the dental field is the scenario of additional emergency procedures during an operation under GA. This is allowed so long as there are clear medical reasons as to WHY such procedures are needed.

Summary of advice on giving consent:

- Find out what the patient wants to know. This means getting to know your patients, including their jobs and interests. Be reassured that, when you are in rapport with people, they generally enjoy talking about themselves. For some people it is their favourite subject!
- If you have any doubt that consent has been obtained, then a cooling off period and another discussion is advisable
- The use of treatment coordinators now carries more risk
- It is not for the clinician to decide what is relevant information
- A blanket policy of telling every patient "everything" is not valid
- There is nothing wrong with developing patient information leaflets to deliver the salient points regarding the risk rewards of treatment, but these are not to be relied on. Relevant discussed information should be added to the treatment plan (possible with FP17DC's???)
- The patient's signature on a piece of paper does not prove their consent
- Information must be bespoke for the individual patient

- Disclaimers and waivers will not remove a patient's right to sue you. You should never do treatment that you do not feel is in the patient's best interests.
- Consent forms, if used, should contain all risks discussed. But why is the consent form no proof of consent? Well in some cases it depends on when the form was signed. As J Popplewell stated in the case **Taylor v Shropshire H.A**[15] *"I regard the consent form immediately before operation as pure window dressing in this case and designed simply to avoid the suggestion that a patient had not been told"*.
- Some would argue that EVERYTHING you say to the patient, and the patient's responses, should be put in the clinical notes. Is your nurse a fast typer? Does she need to be sent on a touch typing course? Is there a risk of repetitive strain injury? Consider a voice recorder during difficult discussions so you can transcribe directly after the appointment. Only the individual clinician can determine how much information they are comfortable recording (see **RECORD KEEPING**).
- However, there is nothing wrong with using pre-printed standard assessment forms to help gather your information for most conversations. Should the case go to the lawyers, what the expert witness wants to see is that you assessed the patient, reached a diagnosis and had a discussion of the pros and cons regarding the different valid options that you believed could deal with the issue.

Consent is a minefield. Although much of it is governed by legislation, there is much that is open to interpretation by the lawyers and the courts. There is also an argument that it is impossible to gain full consent because how do you know a patient has understood what you have said? Despite what the GDC says, the Common law seems to accept there has to be some form of reasonableness behind all this. In the 2006 case of Hamwi v Johnston and The North West London Hospital NHS Trust[16] Justice Simon said the following.

"At one point in her argument, the Claimant's barrister suggested that the clinicians duty is to ensure that the information given to the patient is understood. In my view, that is to place too onerous an obligation on the clinician. It is difficult to see what steps could be devised to ensure that a patient has understood, short of a vigorous and inappropriate cross- examination."

All you can do, in any situation, is your best. And remember, if in doubt, consult your indemnifier.

Your fellow dentist **Shaun Sellars** has created a consent workflow, which I recreate here with permission:

Capacity

Always assume capacity

If in doubt refer to MCA (2005) 2-stage test

Voluntariness

- Ensure consent is gained without coercion
- Coercion can come from practitioner or external source

Patient Dialogue

- Valid consent can only be gained after process of dialogue with patient
- Ask relevant questions - patients can no be expected to volunteer information
- Ensure patient understands:

    - Tx proposed
    - Reasonable alternatives
    - Appropriate Material Risks
    - Benefits
    - Possible negative Outcomes
    - All Associated Costs
- Ensure pt understands consequences of not undergoing tx
- Have individualised consent form signed
- Remember consent can be withdrawn at any time

Knowledge

- Present risks and benefits to patient
- 2 limbed "material risk test"
    - The risk in relation to a reasonable patient in specific circumstances
    - The risk in relation to specific patient in specific circumstances
- Risk should include:
- Commonly occurring poor outcomes of low significance
- Commonly occurring outcomes of high significance
- Uncommon/rare outcomes of high significance to the reasonable patient
- Uncommon/rare outcomes of high significance to the specific patients
- Significance and risk is determined by the patient. Consider specific patient circumstances when discussing risk.
- Theoretical risks may be omitted if irrelevant
- Benefits of recommended tx and all other reasonable treatment options should be explained and discussed
- Cost of each treatment option should be discussed
- No treatment is always a valid option

- Patients are entitled to choose whichever tx option they desire

Consent References:

1. **Mental Health Act Code of Practice 1983** - https://www.gov.uk/government/news/new-mental-health-act-code-of-practice
2. **Chatterton v Gerson [1981] I All ER 257**
3. **Border V Lewisham and Greenwich NHS Trust [2015] ewca civ 8** - http://www.bailii.org/
4. **CQC Regulation 11** - http://www.cqc.org.uk/guidance-providers/regulations-enforcement/regulation-11-need-consent#full-regulation
5. **Children Act 1989** - https://www.legislation.gov.uk/ukpga/1989/41/contentshttps://www.legislation.gov.uk/ukpga/1989/41/contents
6. **British medical Association, *Parental Responsibility* (2008)** - https://www.bma.org.uk/advice/employment/ethics/children-and-young-people/parental-responsibility
7. **Gillick v West Norfolk and Wisbech Area Health Authority [1985] 3 All ER 402 at 420, [1986] 1 AC 112** v- http://www.bailii.org/
8. **S Woolley, 'Children of Jehovah's Witnesses and adolescent Jehovah's Witnesses: what are their rights?' (2005) 90 Arch Dis Child 715**
9. **Re A (Minors) (Conjoined Twins: Separation) [2000] Lloyd's Rep Med 425 (CA)** -
10. *Airedale NHS Trust v Bland* [1993] A.C. 789
11. *Re C (A Child) (HIV Testing)* [2000] 2 W.L.R. 270 (FD)
12. **DH, *Seeking Consent: Working with Children* (2001) -** http://webarchive.nationalarchives.gov.uk/+/http://www.dh.gov.uk/en/Publicationsandstatistics/Publications/PublicationsPolicyandGuidance/DH_4007005

13. **BMA Card 8 - Determining 'Best interests'** - https://www.bma.org.uk/advice/employment/ethics/consent/consent-tool-kit/8-determining-best-interests
14. **DPL: Consent** - http://www.dentalprotection.org/docs/librariesprovider4/dental-advice-booklets/dental-advice-booklet-consent-uk-excl-scot.pdf?sfvrsn=10
15. **Taylor v Shropshire H.A [1998] Lloys law reports: Medical 395** - - http://www.bailii.org/
16. Hamwi v Johnston and The North West London Hospital NHS Trust - http://www.bailii.org/

Negligence

The UK is the most dentally litigious country on planet Earth (with perhaps the exception of Israel). It is even more litigious than the USA which has 50% of the world's lawyers. At the same time indemnity costs are starting to spiral, and there are more and more cases of registrants being "abandoned" by their indemnifiers.

There is also the perception that the indemnifiers "just settle" at the earliest opportunity, passing on the costs to their members. Sometimes, patients seek out lawyers not for the money, but so they can learn what went wrong. It would be disheartening to me if this kind of litigation happened to a UK dentist, because really we should be open and honest with our patients, and indeed this usually occurs with hospital care.

As always, the GDC have something to say on the matter in their standards:

1.8 You must have appropriate arrangements in place for patients to seek compensation if they have suffered harm
Guidance
1.8.1 You must have appropriate insurance or indemnity in place to make sure your patients can claim any compensation to which they may be entitled (See our website for further guidance on what types of insurance or indemnity the GDC considers to be appropriate). **Comment** - indemnity is usually discretionary and there have been several cases where indemnifiers have "acted in the interests of their members" and have left registrants without the promised legal cover for GDC hearings. There have also been registrants who were abandoned by the indemnifiers due to their discretionary nature (this is not a criticism by the way, the indemnifiers are mutual organisations. As that great philosopher

Mr Spock once said, "the needs of the many outweigh the needs of the few").

1.8.2 You should ensure that you keep to the terms and conditions of your insurance or indemnity and contact the provider as soon as possible when a claim is made. A delay in contacting the provider could disadvantage patients and may affect the level of help you receive from the provider

The purpose of an action in negligence is to ensure that the claimant is "no worse off" having suffered from the breach of duty. The whole idea is not to financially reward the claimant, but to provide him with the financial position to be "put back to how he was." This is why for a lost tooth, the lawyers will always claim the cost of an implant for example.

For a patient to have a chance of making a claim in negligence they must first pass four tests, and it is for the patient (the claimant) to prove their case. They must prove there was a duty of care, that the duty of care was breached, that the breach resulted in harm, and that the harm resulted in loss.

Duty of care

When do you have a duty of care towards a patient? If you have been seeing them for many years, it can be implied that you have an ethical duty of care to look after them, but what does the law specifically state? It is important to remember that an ethical obligation is not a legal obligation.

The duty of care actually depends firstly on whether the patient is being seen under NHS contract or privately. The NHS patient is owed a duty of care under Tort, whereas a private patient will be owed a duty under both tort and contract law. It is also important to note that, if it can be proved that you did not obtain adequate consent for the treatment, ANY patient may be able to make a claim in the tort of battery.

The duty of care is made up of different components such as the duty to diagnose, the duty to inform, the duty to treat safely etc. Failure in any of these risks an accusation of a failure in the duty of care. The people who owe the duty are all those directly involved in the patient's care. This would include the dentist, the dental nurse and other clinical staff. There is also an argument that the Principal could be held vicariously liable under the duty for the actions of non-clinical staff.

When does the duty of care begin and end?

When the duty of care is actually established can be difficult to ascertain. Some would argue it is established when you first examine the individual as a patient. This isn't quite right however. As a dentist, you do not owe a duty of care to the "average commuter on the Clapham omnibus". So if a stranger was to stop and ask you for dental advice in the middle of the street, there is no duty of care established and you do not have to respond. If you did respond however, if you proceeded to give advice then there is an argument that a duty of care has been established. This is why I never give advice to anyone outside a clinical setting (except for my Mum lol). But when exactly does the transition from "stranger" to "patient" take place?

The common law answer is when you as a clinician have assumed responsibility for the patient's care. That's a little vague when you think about it. Is it when the patient first makes an appointment or steps across the threshold for their first appointment? Or is it when the patient is first examined and the dentist says the words "you know I think we can help you". It might seem like a burning question, but it is one ultimately for the legal profession to decide. If you never saw the patient, it would be highly unlikely for a case of negligence to proceed due to the following tests that would need to be met.

There is also the matter of figuring out when the duty of care ends. Some would say "when the treatment is finished", but it might not be as simple as that. Here are some examples

1) You refer the patient to secondary care. You will have a duty to make sure that the referral reaches its destination and that at least the patient has been offered an appointment. Should the patient be referred back to you, you will also have a duty to do any follow on treatment that you agree with. There is also a regulatory duty in this regard, especially if you are the dentist being referred to. GDC standard 6.4.2 states: *If you do not think that what you have been asked to do is appropriate, you should discuss this with the colleague who asked you to do it.*
2) If the patient pays privately into a monthly payment plan, there is a strong argument they are entering into a contract with you for continuing care. You will be responsible therefore for doing whatever you can to ensure they return to your practice at the designated recall interval, as well as seeing such patients in an emergency. There will likely be a provision for you to provide some kind of emergency care through the payment plan provider.
3) If the patient is seen on a private basis in a private practice, the duty of care exists whilst the treatment is being done. Once completed, there is an argument that the duty is finished until you agree to next see them again unless you specifically state otherwise. It could be reasonably argued that you have a moral and ethical duty

to provide for them in between recall periods should they need you, but it might be difficult to claim a legally defined duty unless you had entered into some sort of contract, or had specifically stated that such a duty existed. During that treatment phase, the GDC strongly imply you have an out of hours' duty - *2.3.9 You must provide patients with clear information about your arrangements for emergency care including the out of hours' arrangements.* Whilst technically the patients can attend the local NHS emergency cover it would probably be unwise to go down this route.

4) The situation for NHS patients is actually seemingly clear cut. The 2006 contract stipulates the exact hours you are allowed to provide NHS care, and with the exception of your written agreement to provide out of hours' care (usually through an additional mini contract), out of hours' care is to be provided by the Local Area Teams and NHS England. No longer do you have to sit at home awaiting the inevitable call at 21.59 on a Friday night. Your duty of care exists during your surgery hours whilst the individual is a patient of the practice.

Does a duty of care exist with an NHS patient after the treatment is finished (the contract even stipulates what a course of treatment is)? Like with private patients there is a moral and ethical duty, but once the form is sent off to the NHSBSA, it could be argued that the duty ends. The definition of a patient in the 2006 contract is

"patient" means, unless the context otherwise requires, a person to whom the contractor is providing services under the contract.

The NHS contract tells what you can provide and when you can provide it:

(2) A contractor must provide to its patients, during the period specified in paragraph (3), all proper and necessary dental care and treatment which includes—

(a) the care which a dental practitioner usually undertakes for a patient and which the patient is willing to undergo;
(b) treatment, including urgent treatment; and
(c) where appropriate, the referral of the patient for advanced mandatory services, domiciliary
services, sedation services or other relevant services provided under Part 1 of the Act.

(3) A contractor must provide—

(a) urgent treatment; and
(b) all other services described in paragraph (2),
that are necessary to meet the reasonable needs of its patients during normal surgery hours.

(4) The dental care and treatment referred to in paragraph (2) includes—

(a) examination;
(b) diagnosis;
(c) advice and planning of treatment;
(d) preventative care and treatment;
(e) periodontal treatment;
(f) conservative treatment;
(g) surgical treatment;
(h) supply and repair of dental appliances;
(i) the taking of radiographs;
(j) the supply of listed drugs and listed appliances; and
(k) the issue of prescriptions,
but it does not include additional services

The contract is written by lawyers, and so everything in it has a meaning and a purpose. It's point 3 that stipulates that NHS care is only to be during surgery hours. And section 2 stipulates that you must only provide treatment to patient's, patients being someone to whom you are providing services. So once the treatment is complete, is the patient still a patient? Well part 6, schedule 3 might give us some clue to that

Schedule 3

1.—(1) Subject to sub-paragraphs (3) and (5), the contractor may agree to provide mandatory or additional services under the contract to any person if a request is made for such services by—

(a) the person who requires the services; or

(b) a person specified in sub-paragraph (2), on behalf of the person who requires those services.

(3) The contractor may refuse to provide mandatory or additional services in relation to a person falling outside a specified group of persons only where the contract provides for the contractor to provide such services to a specified group.

(4) The contractor shall only refuse to provide services under the contract to a person if it has reasonable grounds for doing so which do not relate to—

(a) a person's race, gender, social class, age, religion, sexual orientation, appearance, disability or medical or dental condition; or

(b) a person's decision or intended decision to accept or refuse private services in respect of himself or a family member.

So as long as you have reasonable grounds (for example you are at capacity, although the meaning of capacity has never been legally defined as far as I'm aware) you can technically refuse to see anyone outside of a course of treatment. That will however be for you and your indemnifier to determine. If the wording in contracts was cut and dry, there would be no need for lawyers.

But I've been rattling on about law and guidelines. We shouldn't really need such things to look after our patients. Because they are ours, despite some Local Area Teams claiming they are theirs (I know we are seeing the patients under a contract that can be taken away and tendered to somebody else, so technically the LAT's might be right for NHS care). They come to us, either NHS or private to be looked after, to be cared for. They want us to help them become and stay healthy, and how can we do that without a long term dentist/patient relationship. In an ideal world, it would be for the dentist and the patient to determine, jointly, when the duty of care begins and ends.

Breach of the duty of care

If it can be established that you as a dentist had a duty of care for a patient, then the next hurdle in negligence is for the claimant to prove that you breached that duty. You will all undoubtedly have heard of the **Bolam** case[1]. Bolam was the name of a patient who had voluntarily attended Friern Hospital where he agreed to undergo electro-convulsive therapy. Because he was not given a muscle relaxant and because his body wasn't restrained he suffered severe injuries including a fracture due to his flailing about. He sued the hospital and this became the Bolam case.

Mr Bolams' solicitors argued that he should have been sedated and restrained. However, this was not common practice at the time, and a "reasonable body of opinion" stated that these measures were not routinely needed. In his judgment dismissing the case, Justice McNair stated:

"I myself would prefer to put it this way, that he is not guilty of negligence if he has acted in accordance with a practice accepted as proper by a responsible body of medical men skilled

in that particular art....Putting it the other way round, a man is not negligent, if he is acting in accordance with such a practice, merely because there is a body of opinion who would take a contrary view. At the same time, that does not mean that a medical man can obstinately and pig-headedly carry on with some old technique if it has been proved to be contrary to what is really substantially the whole of informed medical opinion..."

This is where the Bolam test comes from. Under Bolam the defendant just had to show that his actions were in accordance with a responsible body of opinion (even if there were countering opinions). Now I know what you're thinking, that sounds reasonable doesn't it? Well, solicitors, especially those who sue dental professionals, have never liked Bolam, because that hurdle is quite difficult to overcome. Unfortunately, the law moved on (remember that Bolam was in 1957).

In 1984, Bolam was reinforced by the judgement of Lord Scarman in **Maynard Vs West Midlands RHA[2].** In it Lord Scarman basically said if there was a reasonable body of opinion that supported the doctor's actions, it didn't matter if there was a counter opinion because it was accepted that there were differences of opinion in the medical profession. Ah the "good old days".

In 1985, the use of the Bolam test was itself put to the test in **Sidaway v Board of Governors of the Bethlem Royal Hospital[3]**. This case involved a claimant who had suffered from pain in her neck, right shoulder, and arms. Her neurosurgeon took her consent for cervical cord decompression, but did not include in his explanation the fact that in less than 1% of the cases, the said decompression caused paraplegia. She developed paraplegia after the spinal operation. She sued, but although there was a dissenting voice amongst the judges (Lord Scarman) the court found that the Bolam test was the right test for judging the obtaining of consent in this matter. If a reasonable body of opinion would not warn about the 1% risk, then the doctor in question was not negligent. How times have now changed.

The first cracks in the battlements of Bolam came in 1997 with the **Bolitho v City and Hackney Health Authority**[4] case. Bolitho was a 2-year-old boy who was admitted to hospital with croup. When the child's condition worsened, one of the doctors overseeing the care did not attend and the child stopped breathing. Although revived he suffered brain damage and later died. It was alleged that the doctor should have attended to intubate the child. But it was argued that, even if the doctor had attended, she would not have intubated and that such a decision conformed with a reasonable body of opinion. The judges found for the defendant.

The importance of this ruling revolved around the legitimacy of expert witness evidence. No longer would expert evidence just be accepted. It needed to be rational and logical, consistent and defensible when cross examined. This case began to push the courts above the medical profession in the battle between who became the ultimate arbiters of what was negligence.

This basically changed things to become the Bolam and Bolitho test. Your defence needed to be that a logical and reasonable body of opinion would support your approach.

But things changed again, as they always do. It is important at this stage to introduce to you, the dear distressed and harassed reader, to the concept of "**res ipsa loquitur**", or as you speak English. "**the mere occurrence of an accident is sufficient to imply negligence**". In dental context, a good example of this would be extracting the UR6 when it was the UL6 that needed taking out. There can be no excuse and no defence for such an incident, and it would be a challenge for any expert witness to say anything but the obvious truth in such an occurance. Bolam and Bolitho can give no defense for such an occasion. But I digress. Perhaps pour yourself another glass of that lovely 2013 Merlot. We might be a while.

In the 1999 case, Brooks V Home Office[5] the standard of care available was brought into question. An incarcerated pregnant woman, it was determined, should receive the same level of care as someone free to roam. Although this was stated, it was determined that the still birth of the claimant's child was not caused by a delay in accessing care and the case was thrown out. However, this helped establish the principle that it is generally considered proper that like be compared with like. Thus the root filling of a GDP should not be viewed as comparable with the root filling of a specialist. A GDP should reach the standards of a competent GDP. A specialist should reach the standard of a competent specialist. That being said, the 1993 case of **Bull V Devon AHA**[6] highlighted that a basic standard of care should always be met.

The defence of inexperience unfortunately does not amount to much in the world of litigation. In **Wilsher V Essex AHA**[7] it was stated that a junior doctor owed the same standard of care as an experienced fully qualified doctor. Once you as a GDP (for example) claim that you are capable of doing treatment X, you will be judged against the level expected of a reasonably competent GDP. In a hospital environment, the usual procedure is for the junior dentist to consult and seek the supervision of a senior colleague until the competence level reaches a desirable standard. But how does this work in a busy primary care dental practice? Even the GDC point out that you should only work within your competency… but how does one gain competency without first performing the tasks? Many a dental graduate has been failed by their dental school by graduating without the prerequisite knowledge of all kinds of treatments. Perhaps this is one of the reasons Vocational Training was developed. Who knows?

There are some who would say, in light of this, that partaking in costly and advanced treatments after going to Heathrow to do a weekend Short Term ortho course/ Implant course might perhaps best be put into the realms of "something we used to do".

It is a clear fact that you learn from your mistakes, and that the more you do, the more mistakes you make, thus allowing you to adapt and mould your technique until experience turns you into a competent individual. You do not learn to drive by sitting at home reading the Highway code. Unfortunately, our adversarial legal and regulatory system now makes perfecting our art a challenge. The positive rise in the value of mentoring and the negative rise in the habit of young graduates to refer anything that seems risky is a reflection of this.

One of the ways the Americans lowered their risk of litigation was to become more and more specialised. The NHS would not be able to fund or accommodate such a development here. But back to the matter at hand because the Wolf is at the door. Lord Woolf to be exact.

In 1999 the **Woolf reforms** were brought in, updating Part 35 of the **Civil Procedure Rules** which governs how expert witnesses have to behave. This laid out, in clear language, that the duty of expert witnesses was to the courts and not the party that paid for their services. It also put a limit on what expert witnesses could be paid for their evidence and testimony, and pushed for more use of joint expert witnesses. Where that was not appropriate, it was made very clear how expert witnesses were to discuss the case to try and reach a consensus with limited input from the solicitors.

The days of the biased expert witness were supposed to be at an end, although several cases at a certain regulator within the last five years have shown the inherent bias that lurks within some expert witnesses… who perhaps did not understand their remit. To their credit, this has actually prompted reforms at the GDC and they are taking measures to combat this bias.

You may find it hard to believe that there are some dentists who will go out of their way to be critical of their fellow professionals, either in the role of dentist or expert witness. Actually I suspect you don't find that hard to believe at all. I will leave you to make your own judgement about such individuals because I couldn't possibly comment.

Montgomery[8]

Jesus Steve, why are you always going on about Montgomery? Because it has the potential to be a game changer (maybe not for dentists, but for the overall medical profession). For dentists, Montgomery put into common law what already existed in regulation. Here's what the GDC have been saying since 2013:

2.3.2 Other members of your team may have valuable knowledge about the patients' backgrounds or concerns so you should involve them (and the patients' carers if relevant) in discussion with patients where appropriate.
2.3.3 You should recognise patients' communication difficulties and try to meet the patients' particular communication needs by, for example:

- ***not using professional jargon and acronyms;***
- ***using an interpreter for patients whose first language is not English;***

- ***suggesting that patients bring someone with them who can use sign language;***
- ***and providing an induction loop to help patients who wear hearing aids.***

2.3.4 You should satisfy yourself that patients have understood the information you have given them, for example by asking questions and summarising the main points of your discussion.
2.3.5 You should make sure that patients have enough information and enough time to ask questions and make a decision.

In my day we called this co-diagnosis. In a way it could be argued that it was inevitable for Montgomery to happen because the medics (and to an extent some dentists) are really behind the times in regards to this. Although Australian, the case of **Roger Vs Whitaker**[9] was a warning of the way the wind was starting to blow. This case, a landmark in the Australian legal system, ascertained that a risk was material if a reasonable person would attach significance to it.

The truth is, you can't have such a highly litigious system and a situation where doctors don't give their patients the information they need. The two just don't go together. It's like oil and water. The cracks in the dam had been getting ever bigger and something had to give. Unfortunately, it wasn't the litigious nature of our society that changed.

Montgomery is an important ruling because it deals with consent, and as you probably know by now, if you don't have consent, it doesn't matter how good a clinician you are. At the end of the day, treatment without consent risks an accusation of battery. Perhaps the essence of Montgomery is captured in this extract from the ruling:

"The doctor's advisory role involves dialogue, the aim of which is to ensure that the patient understands the seriousness of her condition, and the anticipated benefits and risks of the proposed treatment and any reasonable alternatives, so that she is then in a position to make an informed decision. This role will only be performed effectively if the information provided is comprehensible. The doctor's duty is not therefore fulfilled by bombarding the patient with technical information which she cannot reasonably be expected to grasp, let alone by routinely demanding her signature on a consent form."

Bolam no longer applies when it comes to consent. Whereas before it was what the reasonable dentist thought s/he should warn about, now it is all about what the reasonable patient would want to know. So what exactly happened in Montgomery? Basically the essence of the case is that a pregnant woman gave birth to a baby with cerebral palsy, caused by a brachial plexy injury and compression of the umbilical chord (due to shoulder dystocia, a recognised risk of a diabetic mother) and that if she had been warned of such she would have opted for a caesarean section.

Medical litigation cases involving consent issues prior to this had actually been relatively rare, and Bolam/Bolitho had generally been applied in such cases. Not so in Montgomery v Lanarkshire Health Board. So where are we now? Basically the situation is that you, as a clinician, need to find out what your patient wants to know about the treatment. Unfortunately, this does not mean that you can go down the American model and give them a 27-page document of all the possible risks. That won't wash. Montgomery has introduced a new test:

"The test of materiality is whether, in the circumstances of the particular case, a reasonable person in the patient's position

would be likely to attach significance to the risk, or the doctor is or should reasonably be aware that the particular patient would be likely to attach significance to it"

As Philippa White remarked in her article "10":

"Montgomery fundamentally shifts the balance of power with regard to information giving and consent. Patients are now entitled to receive any information they ask for in order to make their own decisions, regardless of whether the health professional would usually explain the nature of the information to the patient. Save for limited circumstances, this is also regardless of any professional judgement as to whether the information is relevant. The default position is now that information to be shared is 'what the patient wants to know' not 'what the health professional wants to tell'. The 'prudent patient' has arrived."

The thing is, in an ideal world this case should never come about, because like the GDC, the GMC have been advising this approach to consent since 1995 according to some authors[11]. It was certainly the case that the GMC were advocating this since 2008 in their guidance **Good Medical Practice and Consent: Patients and Doctors Making Decisions Together**[12].

It gets better however. This new common law is retrospective, and could possibly apply for as far back as 1999 (the date Mrs Montgomery gave birth). It will also make consent a major issue in future litigation, which worryingly introduces the tort of battery into the mix. Remember breach of duty is not about something going wrong per se, more that it was outside the expected standard of care. In complex biological systems like the human body things don't always go according to plan, despite your best efforts.

So in summary for treatment to be in line with the standard of care so that you do not breach your duty:

- Your treatment should be logical and in line with accepted dental practice
- The practice itself must be current. Whilst you won't be expected to know of every single new guideline and treatment recommendation, you are expected to keep up to date (this is a GDC requirement don't forget).
- A reasonable body of opinion should agree that your treatment is sound and justified
- You must have full consent in line with Montgomery
- Your treatment should normally follow the guidelines set out by your regulator and by bodies such as NICE and FGDP. That being said you are not expected to follow guidelines if you KNOW this will result in harm for the patient. Guidelines are strong suggestions that you are allowed to alter if you have good clinical justification for doing so.
- A GDP is expected to practice at the level of a reasonably capable GDP, i.e. what a reasonable and responsible group of dentists with similar skills to the defendant would or would not have done

The good news in all this is that, even if you are found to have a duty of care that you have breached, there are still more hurdles for the patient to jump over. This is known as the test of causation.

Causation

After the claimant has shown that a duty of care exists and that the duty has been breached, they must then show that the dentist's lack of care caused the injuries. In other words, it must be shown that foreseeable damage was suffered by the patient, and that said damage has a definite link to the breach of duty.

The technical term used by many is that the breach of duty caused harm (damage, pain and suffering etc) and caused loss. Sometimes (for example squirting hypochlorite through the end of the tooth) this is easy to ascertain. Other times it is not so clear cut. It is not sufficient to simply prove breach of duty. The classic example of this would be a 15-year-old root filling that was done without rubber dam and is well short of the clinical length. If the tooth is sign and symptom free and can be left, the patient has not suffered any harm or loss and so will be unlikely to succeed in a claim for negligence. It is also important to note that allegations of causation will, if the case goes to trial, ultimately be decided by a judge. The allegation isn't necessarily the outcome.

This is where we introduce the "**But For**" test - But for the dentist's negligence, the claimant would not have suffered damage. The negligent act must have directly caused or materially contributed to the injury or condition claimed for. There are several aspects that need to be taken into account:

1) Did the breach of duty materially contribute to the damage?

Sometimes there can be more than one cause of damage. Was it the poor technique in bonding the veneer, or the fact that the patient was punched in the face Friday night that shattered the veneer? This comes from the Bonnington test:

In **Bonnington Castings V Wardlow**[13] the claimant suffered pneumoconiosis due to the dust produced in the job he did. This dust was in excess to that naturally present in the work process (remember this was 1956). Whilst it couldn't be determined which of the two types of dust caused the condition, it was ruled that the excess dust "materially contributed to the disease". So if you did a root filling without rubber dam, without doing say a working length estimation and the root filling subsequently failed, the claimant would be trying to show that your failure to adhere to the required standards/procedures (as would be expected from a reasonably competent GDP) materially contributed to the root filling failure. There might have been other plausible reasons why the root filling could have failed, but all the claimant has to show is that the dentist materially contributed to the harm and loss.

2) Did the breach of duty materially increase the risk?

Again the common law applies, as seen in the case of **McGhee v N.C.B**[14]. The claimant developed dermatitis from his job, the employer failing to provide adequate washing facilities, thus significantly increasing the risk of dermatitis developing. So if you failed to diagnose the patient's high caries rate and act accordingly, it could be argued that this materially increased the risk of further treatment being required.

3) Loss of Chance

This is quite a complicated issue and relates to hypothetical outcomes. Loss of chance relates to a pre-existing condition. Due to the negligence, the claimant loses the chance to make a full recovery. In other words, **the possible becomes the inevitable**. Your failure to spot an early presenting squamous cell carcinoma denied the claimant the opportunity of early intervention. However, to succeed the claimant would need to show to the court that there was at least a 51% likelihood that they would have made a complete recovery if it were not for the dentist's breach of duty. They must prove this on the balance of probability, and should they be unsuccessful, the claimant would not be entitled to a percentage of the damages sought. It's a bit like a TV game show when they put everything on the line for that "special" prize. It has to be all or nothing.

4) The Chain of Causation

This refers to the linked series of events, leading from breach of duty to damage and loss. If the chain can be broken by an event or third party not related to the dentist, then it may be possible to defend the accusation of causation.

Contract law

Whilst NHS patients are not allowed to seek redress under contract law, private patients are. A private patient will have an implied contract that their dentist will perform their treatment with "reasonable skill and care." So long as you did the treatment to a level that is supported by a reasonable body of opinion, a patient would find it difficult to sue you via this route.

Unless....

Some private dentists give guarantees, either written, verbal or implied. And if the patient feels that the guarantee was not met, they may have a means to go after you under contract law. Remember under contract law, the patient does not have to apply the four negligence tests, just that you breached the promised contract. There are also several advantages in suing under contract:

- **A simple claim in contract can be taken 6 years after the breach occurs**
- **It may be possible to claim higher damages under contract law. Generally, the purpose of damages for breach of contract is the same as with negligence.**
- **It is generally considered easier to bring a "loss of chance" claim under contract than under negligence**

So if you are going to offer guarantees, they have to be very specific, in writing and preferably very limited. My personal view is you shouldn't offer them at all.

Defences to Litigation

Short of not actually being negligent under Bolam/Bolitho and Montgomery, there are three other defences that may come into play when faced with litigation:

1) Consent

This is a general defence in Tort. If you consent to an action being done, how can you then go on to sue someone who did as you asked? Let us say you take out a tooth after giving the patient the options of XLA or RCT, as long as you can prove you had the patient's consent, they should not then be able to come back at you and claim you shouldn't have taken the tooth out. This is also the consent to accept the risks associated with the procedure. Hence the warning of tongue and lip numbness when one takes out a lower eight. Remember with Montgomery, you need to relay the information in a way the patient will understand, and should it go to trial, it will be for the Judge to determine if valid consent was obtained.

2) Contributory Negligence:

Until recently this wasn't a defence that was often used, but it will be up to the judge to decide what, if any, reduction in the amount awarded should apply. The principle is that, although the dentist was negligent, the patient's actions contributed to the injury. An easy example would be a patient smoking after an extraction (that had been deemed as falling below the standard of care) with resultant post-operative complications. It could be argued that the smoking broke down the clot and contributed to the subsequent issues.

3) Limitation.

This is covered by the **Limitation act 1980**[15]. As has already been stated, there is a time limit for litigation. For negligence, the time period is three years from injury or three years from when the patient became aware of the injury. If the patient tries to open an action more than 3 years after the actual treatment was done, the defence of limitation will be by trying to prove that the patient was informed of the complications they are now complaining of at the time.

So basically to use the defence of Limitation, the defendant would have to show proof that the patient was informed of the incident, that the incident was significant and that it was whole or in part the result of the injury being claimed for. So take the scenario of you fracturing off a file during your endo because you had been a little bit over enthusiastic with your rotaries. If you informed the patient of the issue, gave options on how to deal with it (referral etc) and documented the discussion, if the tooth flared up five years later you might have a defence. But then the court might make an exception. It's not guaranteed because there is a lot of ambiguity when it comes to case law in this matter. Don't rely on it because it will be for the judges and the lawyers to determine. Of course if you didn't warn the patient about what went wrong, then the clock starts ticking from when they are told. Do you see why it is beneficial to be open and honest in your dealings with patients? But when it comes to what constitute "knowledge" on the patient's part of a negligent act, whole books have been written on the matter.

In regards to this the Limitation Act states the following in section 14:

(1) This section applies to any action for damages for negligence, other than one to which section 11 of this Act applies, where the starting date for reckoning the period of limitation under subsection (4)(b) below falls after the date on which the cause of action accrued.

....

(4) That period is either—

(a)six years from the date on which the cause of action accrued; or

(b)three years from the starting date as defined by subsection (5) below, if that period expires later than the period mentioned in paragraph (a) above. **(applies to negligence)**

(5) For the purposes of this section, the starting date for reckoning the period of limitation under subsection (4)(b) above

is the earliest date on which the plaintiff or any person in whom the cause of action was vested before him first had both the knowledge required for bringing an action for damages in respect of the relevant damage and a right to bring such an action.

In addition to the court's discretion, there are also definite exceptions to the 3-year rule. For under 18's, the clock doesn't start ticking until they reach the age of 18. Think of all that ortho that starts to relapse around the age of 20. And for adults who are deemed not to have capacity, the clock only starts ticking down once capacity has been re-established (see the chapter on CONSENT for capacity issues).

A warning to practice owners

Registration with the CQC and GDC guidance gives the practice principal a degree of control over the associates working under him. Whilst they may claim to be self-employed and self-indemnified, they also work in an environment provided and staffed by the principal. They treat patients that are organised and booked in by the principal's employees whilst often wearing clothing and using equipment provided by the principal. The associate contract, whilst implying self-employed status, also often stipulates the amount of holidays that can be taken, as well as other restrictions normally only reserved for employees. Also, NHS UDA contracts are not contracts with individual associates, but with practice owners, and associates working there are expected to be compliant with the policies and procedures of the practice, especially when it comes to clinical governance. The associate, whilst being allowed a modicum of clinical freedom, has little say in how the practice is run and generally is obliged to use the materials provided to him/her unless they are allowed to buy their own. Can such an associate claim s/he is an independent business working in your premises?

Recent case law has opened up the possibility that all practice Principals may be vicariously liable for the actions of their associates. Although technically self-employed in the eyes of HMRC, there have been several legal cases moving the landscape in this direction, and in 2012 the Court of Appeal in **E v English Province of Our Lady of Charity**[16] ruled that an employer may well be liable for an associate's (in this instance a priest) negligence if the employer stands in a relationship that is "akin to employment" with that associate (and if the lawyers are saying this, how long do you think it will be before HMRC come for their pound of flesh?). In doing so they introduced a new test which again in 2012 was approved by the Supreme Court in **Various Claimants v Catholic Child Welfare Society**[17].

This was later reinforced in 2013 in the case **Woodland v Essex County Council**[18] when the judge found that a hospital has a direct liability and a vicarious liability to the patients treated. A further 2014 High Court case, **Whetstone V MPS**[19] initially sent shock waves through the profession. Mr Whetstone, a practice principal, "employed" an associate who it later turned out worked in the practice for several years without indemnity. The associate was referred to the GDC by Mr Whetstone regarding "*care and treatment [which was] inadequate*". The allegations to the GDC related to 19 patients and the GDC erased the associate from the dental register. Whetstone then took the unusual path of writing to a bunch of his patients, informing them of the situation. In the letter he admitted liability for the associate's work and advised the patients to sue him rather than the associate so that Mr Whetstone could call on the defences of his own indemnifier, Dental Protection Ltd. Mr Whetstone was offering to fix all the negligent work but was allegedly expecting his own indemnifier to pay him for it. When the matter went to court, MPS won (which considering their cover is discretionary was pretty much inevitable). But in the victory the following was stated by Judge Seymour:

"In the result I find that Mr. Whetstone is vicariously liable to the claimants in action [case number] for the negligent treatment of them by [the associate]."

Judge Seymour also mentioned the "akin to employment" test in his ruling. This test will be met when certain criteria are found:

(i) the employer is more likely to have the means to compensate the victim than the employee and can be expected to have insured against that liability;

(ii) the tort will have been committed as a result of activity being taken by the employee on behalf of the employer;

(iii) the employee's activity is likely to be part of the business activity of the employer;

(iv) the employer, by employing the employee to carry on the activity will have created the risk of the tort committed by the employee;

(v) the employee will, to a greater or lesser degree, have been under the control of the employer

This was not a case of an indemnifier abandoning one of their members. To quote DPL on the matter:

"In a sense, Mr Whetstone was seeking to profit from his associate's lack of indemnity and his own failure to check that suitable arrangements were in place".[20]

Whetstone and Woodland might be seen to make principals responsible and legally liable for the negligent actions of their associates (DPL have stated this isn't the case and state they can give guidance on how to structure an associate contract to minimise such a risk). A more recent case might have even solidified this situation further. In the 2017 case **Various Claimants v Barclays Bank PLC**[21], Barclays Bank was found vicariously liable for a doctor they engaged to conduct staff medical examinations. The doctor died in 2009 but the police later opened numerous cases to investigate accusations of sexual impropriety on behalf of the doctor. The matter went to court and Barclays lost, the bank being held vicariously liable for the actions of its self-employed contractor.

Would this apply to negligence? I think the wind is definitely blowing that way and the matter still seems to be open to debate in the legal profession. Ultimately, as this is a common law issue, the matter will be decided, one way or the other by a judge's ruling. Whilst it will be more than likely for a patient to seek redress from the dentist who treated them, should that dentist "disappear" or have a lack of indemnity, the principal of the practice should prepare themselves for the possibility of a claim. This then begs the question as to whether the "discretionary" indemnifiers would be there for the principal. Only the indemnifiers themselves could answer that.

What you have to remember about the common law is that nothing is definite until a judge has made his ruling, and even then that ruling can be overturned by higher courts. Very few things are ever cut and dry.

How does litigation proceed

Litigation is controlled by the Civil Procedure Rules (CPR)[22]. These set out the rules and processes that must be followed for litigation to go ahead. Before this though, the patient must raise the matter with a solicitor. The patient will meet with the solicitor to outline what they believed happened. The solicitor will take a detailed statement from the patient and ascertain what the patient wants.

An apology or compensation?

If the patient has sought other advice, such as PALS or the Citizens Advice Bureau, the solicitor will want to see copies of this correspondence. The solicitor will want to know:

- The names of the dental staff involved and the practice address
- What communication occurred between the patient and dentist, including whether an official complaint has been made. If so, who did the patient complain to?
- What treatment was done and whether there were any witnesses (family members etc)
- The dates the treatment was done
- What happened with the treatment
- The patient's full medical history
- The specifics of why the patient thinks the dentist and/or his staff were negligent. Did anyone (another dentist for example) say anything to indicate that negligence exists

It is at this visit that the solicitor (if they believe the case has merit) will discuss the funding of the case. It is worth taking a moment to go through exactly how cases of litigation can be paid for by the patient, as the costs are high. In 2010 Lord Jackson[23] reviewed the cost of civil litigation and determined that there was scope to decrease the cost involved in litigation. Many of his recommendations were adopted in the 2013 **Civil Justice Reforms**, but it is not in the scope of this book to discuss them because the reforms would make up a magnum opus in their own right.

Funding and costs of litigation

Whilst the court does have discretion over costs, it is generally accepted that the losing party will pay the other sides costs. There are limitations to this which will be discussed shortly. Many people will also be surprised to find that legal aid is generally not available for civil negligence cases, so to bring a case it will need to be funded by other means. The patient can self-fund with the hope of claiming back the money through a winning case. This is usually outside the scope of most people, as costs can quickly spiral so is rarely undertaken. Most patient's will pursue litigation using what is called a "Conditional Fee Agreement" (CFA).

Conditional fee agreement (CFA's)

CFA's were brought into life in 1995 by the **Conditional Fees Agreements Regulations**[24]. Initially limited in scope, the scope of their use was extended over the subsequent years (some reports say as a means to help replace legal aid). Under a CFA the solicitor and the patient agree to share the risk of litigation. A CFA is a legal funding arrangement where the patient agrees that the solicitor will charge an enhanced fee if they win the case. This way the solicitor agrees to not be paid until the successful completion of the case. The patient only pays when the case is successful, and only when the patient has received the compensation, with the understanding that the patient will not have to pay their solicitor any direct fees if the case is lost. The success fee, usually 25%, is paid out of the compensation awarded to the patient.

So if the patient loses, are they still not faced with a mind numbing bill because surely they are liable for the defence costs and the expert witness fees? Not only would they have to face the prospect of paying the fees of the rejoicing dentist, but also the disbursements (third party fees such as expert witnesses) paid out by their own solicitor. Well firstly, solicitors will generally only enter into a CFA if they think they will win and if they think it will be worth their time. So if Mrs Miggins doesn't like her NHS denture that you made for her, and she's been edentulous for 40 years, a lawyer is probably not going to be interested because there isn't going to be that much of an upside to it all. But if you are one of those muppets who doesn't know what a BPE probe is and Mrs Miggins starts losing teeth due to the perio you failed to diagnose, the lawyers are probably going to add you to their Christmas card list.

See, you just made a new friend.

Also not many lawyers relish the prospect of working for free, nor do they relish the prospect of trying to recover costs from someone with limited means. Occasionally existing insurance policies (for example home insurance) will have "Bolt On" extras that can fund litigation. But this **Before the Event** (BTE) insurance is quite rare for clinical negligence.

So along comes **After the Event** (ATE) insurance, policies to aid with things that had actually already happened. Some ATE's are even organised so the premiums need only be paid at the end of the case. In the event the case is lost, this pays the opponents fees up to a designated value. If the case wins, the cost of the insurance is NOT paid by the losing side however.

So as long as the patient wins, they really have none of their own money to pay to anyone because it can all come from what the court awards them. And if they lose, they pay only the insurance so long as it covers all the costs. This is not to say that the use of insurance is fool proof. Clinical negligence cases can by high risk for both sides with a likelihood of high costs (despite the government's half-hearted attempts to reduce them). Because of this the premium for ATE insurance can be quite high, more than some people can actually afford, ranging from hundreds to thousands of pounds depending on the complexity of the cases. And paying the premium for the insurance can often be deferred and even paid for with a loan. But said insurance seems to be sufficient to keep the momentum of dental litigation ever upward. ATE insurance can also, in some cases cover the cost of expert witness fees.

So much for an end to no "win no fee".

With this interview done the solicitor will get the patient to check the draft of what will become the "patient's proof of evidence". In addition to this more paperwork will be needed. This is why the lawyers charge the big bucks, filling in forms is dangerous work. The extra paperwork includes:

- Getting the patient to complete a form of authority so that the requested parties can release the dental records
- Forward the patient a care letter as per Solicitors Practice Rule 15
- Highlight any special circumstances (children, those who lack consent etc)
- Determine the limitation period

Pre-Action Protocol[25]

Once the solicitor is satisfied there is a case and that the case can be funded they will engage in the next step. This involves following what are called the Pre-Action Protocols (PAP's). Under the protocol the solicitor will write to the dentist (the Preliminary Notice) and make a request for any and all clinical records relating to the alleged negligence. To do this they will have needed to include written permission from the patient for the disclosure of those records (remember the importance of confidentiality). The records should be processed within 40 days, and this is definitely when you should get your defence organisation involved (if not sooner if the patient has complained or you suspect that they may sue). Your indemnifier will assist in all issues, assuming you are not one of the select few that such organisations occasionally abandon (this is normally still quite rare, but tends to get a lot of air time on social media). It is usual to act through your indemnifier. Sending them all the correspondence and allowing them to be your intermediary with the patient's solicitors.

As has already been shown, the patient has almost unfettered access to their records. This access is provided in law by the **Access to Personal files Act**, the Access to **Medical Reports Act**, the **Data Protection Act** and the **Access to Health Records Act** (for records post 1991).

Once they have the notes, the lawyers will go through everything with a fine toothed comb. Most of the specialist dental litigation firms now employ dental advisors to help with this. From this, a series of allegations will be compiled. Often, the allegations and the patient notes will be sent to an expert witness to give an opinion on breach of duty and causation. The Expert must be chosen from the required speciality (a GDP can be an expert, it doesn't have to be a specialist) and a fee agreed beforehand (either an hourly rate or a fixed fee). There are rules for expert witnesses which we will discuss elsewhere in this book. There will be several things the lawyers will ask from the expert witness.

- The solicitor will write to the expert outlining the specifics of the case. What the alleged negligence is etc.
- Lawyers often highlight what the test for negligence is. Perhaps some expert witnesses don't know ☺

- They will ask if the expert can determine from the information provided whether the injury was caused by substandard care. In other words, they will ask whether the expert thinks causation can be proven.
- The lawyers may want to know if there are any pre-existing conditions that may impact the case.
- Whether a physical examination of the patient will be needed
- They will also remind the expert of their requirements under the CPR.

The expert will then write their independent report. That cannot be empathised enough. The report is intended for the courts, not the solicitor that engages the expert, so if the expert feels there is no case s/he is free to say so. An unfavourable report may see a case dropped, or the solicitor may engage another expert if they are convinced of the merit of the case.

The experts report MUST comply with the requirements laid out in the CPR. There are different types of reports

- An opinion report on breach of duty
- An opinion report on causation
- A condition and prognosis report
- A Quantum report

Once the lawyer is happy they will then issue a "Letter of Claim" to the dentist which needs to be responded to within 14-21 days via a "Letter of Acknowledgment". The Letter of Claim can take many months to arrive (many cases are actually dropped at the initial expert witness stage, especially if the notes are full and contemporaneous). The letter of claim will state:

- The case summary

- The allegations
- The summary of the injuries alleged
- The details of any financial loss incurred

The defendant's indemnifier should notify the patient if they feel the letter of claim does not comply with the PAP. A full response can then be organised by the dentist's indemnifier (via expert witness reports etc.), and usually they are given three months to do this. One of three responses will happen from this. The dentist's indemnifier will either

- Issue a letter of Response
- Issue a letter of Settlement
- Or do both

They will either admit the claim in full, deny the claim in full, or outline aspects of the case that are admitted and denied. To do this, the indemnifier will employ an expert witness of their own to give an independent opinion on the matter. In negligence it is usual for both the patient (claimant) and the defence (dentist) to have their own expert witnesses (see EXPERT WITNESSES).

If the expert witnesses from both sides disagree, they will be invited to meet and discuss the matter. Because they are both independent, there is no need for the solicitors to be present. Although the lawyers are allowed to be present, there are strict rules for their conduct. Sometimes the expert witnesses can form an agreement on the issue, in which case they will form a joint statement for the court. A joint agreed witness statement may well force one of the parties to settle. All the time both teams of lawyers will be weighing up the pros and cons of taking the case forward because the further down the road the case goes, the more expensive it will be to the losing side. Also, should the matter go to trial, the court will need to give their permission before expert evidence is relied upon. Because of the complexity of medical negligence cases, it is unlikely that expert evidence will be denied.

If the letter of response denies the claim in full it is then open for the patient to begin court proceedings. In any other circumstances, the two parties should commence negotiations with the aim of resolving the claim in six months. These are often the cases you hear of that have been "settled". Often cases are settled by indemnifiers because, for a variety of reasons, part or all of the case is deemed to be indefensible.

Alternative Dispute Resolution[26]

Obviously if the dentist were to deny the claim it would require the case to go forward. Before that however, the PAP encourages both parties to go to what is known as Alternative Dispute Resolution (ADR), a form of mediation, stating that court proceedings should be considered the last step. There is very good reason for both parties to attempt ADR. Firstly, it's cheaper. Secondly the courts expect this step to be taken, and can actually penalise the parties that don't actively try and engage in mediation. The best way to think of this is that it is as a form of mediation.

ADR should be considered in the following instances:

- Prior to the issue of court proceedings
- After each case management conference
- After a pre-trial review
- Whenever one of the sides offers to take the matter to mediation
- If the Court recommends it

Part 36 offers

What many dentists don't realise is that litigation is now geared towards settlement. The courts much prefer the matter be dealt with outside of their hallowed halls. And each side will only want to go forward where they know they have a strong chance of winning. We often hear of indemnifiers settling case after case, but please know they do this because they feel there is no chance of winning. Often key factors of the case will not be in the tales of woe you read on Facebook. This lack of ability to defend can be due to a variety of reasons. A good, credible witness who has suffered significant harm and loss when faced against a dentist's clinical records that say "Exam, S/P. XLA UR7 TC", often result in cases that cannot be defended in the majority of occasions. The dentist's best defence is good clinical records recording logical treatment that follows existing practice, guidance and protocols... with a good record and display that consent has been obtained.

Part 36 can be made by either party but must be made prior to court proceedings. If a Part 36 offer is made and rejected, the court will be informed of this matter. If a part 36 offer is made by the claimant and rejected and at trial the claimant wins and obtains a judgment that is as favourable as the Part 36 offer they made, the claimant will be able to claim an additional sum from the defendant above that which was rewarded. Likewise, if a patient rejects a Part 36 offer, they too can be penalised.

So as you see, there are very strong reasons to settle where possible. Unfortunately, this does tend to create an environment where a "litigious culture" can thrive. We as professionals must therefore do all we can to make sure the treatment we provide is, at the very least, well recorded and based in sound practice. Just because something went wrong doesn't mean you were negligent per se, but it can become negligent without the information required to defend you.

If after all that no agreement or offer of settlement has been agreed, then it goes to the courts. Only if a claim has a value of more than £50,000 will it go to the High Court, most lower claims going to the County Court. The claimant will complete form N1 which will also need the "particulars of claim" to be attached. The court then issues a claim form and the proceedings start or are "brought" when the claim form is received by the court.

The claim form will then be served on the defendant (you) and this must be done within four months. To defend, the dentist must respond to this claim within 14 days and file his/her defence within another 14 days. The court will allocate the case to one of three tracks, depending on the value of the claim.

Small Claims track	**- Claim less than £1000**
Fast track claim	**- Less than £15,000**
Multi track claim	**- More than £15,000, or particularly complex cases (majority of dental negligence)**

Trial

Once a case goes before the court then it's usually because both sides think they are going to win. It is usual for the patient's barrister to be heard first. They give an opening statement that lays out the facts of the case as they see it. Their witnesses will be called, and the patient themselves is likely to give evidence. Here the clinical notes become invaluable. After the patient's barrister has questioned each witness, the defendant's barrister can cross examine, and the evidence of the expert witnesses are usually key. Once the patient's case has been heard, the roles reverse and the defendant now gets to call their witnesses, which will also be cross examined. There will then come closing statements and the Judge will retire to bring his verdict.

The Expert Witness

The role of the expert witness is vital, but often misunderstood by us as dentists and sometimes by the expert witness themselves. The Expert Witness has to act independently, and even has to sign a declaration as such. Unfortunately, as Simon Thackeray (a dentist in the midlands) pointed out in the dissertation for his LLM, it is very easy for expert witnesses to be biased. If you know him, ask him for a copy. It's definitely worth a read. Here is the declaration experts have to make in their evidence

EXPERT'S DECLARATION

- ***I understand that my overriding duty is to the Court, both in preparing reports and in giving oral evidence. I have complied and will continue to comply with that duty.***
- ***I have set out in my report what I understand from those instructing me to be the questions in respect of which my opinion as an expert is required.***
- ***I have done my best, in preparing this report, to be accurate and complete. I have mentioned all matters which I regard as relevant to the opinions I have expressed. All of the matters on which I have expressed an opinion lie within my field of expertise.***
- ***I have drawn attention to all matters, of which I am aware, which might adversely affect my opinion or which might affect the validity of this report. I have addressed this report to the Court and I further understand that my duty to the Court overrides any obligation to the party from whom I received instructions.***

- ***Wherever I have no personal knowledge, I have indicated the source of factual information.***
- ***I have not included anything in this report which has been suggested to me by anyone, including the lawyers instructing me, without forming my own independent view of the matter.***
    - ***Where, in my view, there is a range of reasonable opinion, I have indicated the extent of that range in the report.***
    - ***At the time of signing the report I consider it to be complete and accurate. I will notify those instructing me if, for any reason, I subsequently consider that the report requires any correction or qualification.***
- ***I understand that this report will be the evidence that I will give under oath, subject to any correction or qualification I may make before swearing to its veracity.***
- ***I have included in this report a statement setting out the substance of all facts and instructions given to me which are material to the opinions expressed in this report or upon which those opinions are based.***
- ***I have not been subject to any fitness to practise inquiry, criminal proceedings or other matters either personal or professional which could call into question my standing as an expert.***
- ***I confirm that I am aware of the requirements of Part 35 and Practice Direction 35, and the Guidance for the Instruction of Experts in Civil Claims 2014***

In civil proceedings an expert's evidence is admissible under section 1 of the **Civil Evidence Act 1995.**[27]

There was a time when this declaration didn't need to be made, and there was a time when it was recognised that expert witnesses were often less than impartial in their evidence. The Woolf reforms took measures to put a stop to that, and expert witnesses would be wise not to breach these guidelines. Judges will not tolerate bias if it is uncovered. Not only could they penalise the side the expert witness is giving evidence for, but they can even throw out evidence in its entirety. In a dental negligence case that would be a death knell to a case, whether defence or claimant.

Such actions would have definite repercussions on the expert witness. Not only could it result in a referral to the GDC, but the expert witness him/herself could be sued. Expert witnesses used to have immunity under a 400 year old understanding, but that was removed in the case of **Jones v Kaney**[28]. It is now strongly advised that expert witnesses have their own insurance to cover this eventuality because it will not be covered by their indemnity. After discussion with the GDC, they have confirmed this lack of immunity extends to GDC expert witnesses.

The rules governing the role of Expert Witnesses in civil cases are set out in Part 35[29] of the Civil Procedure rules which can be found in **Appendix 6**. So what does this mean for you as a dentist. If a case were to go to court or a GDC fitness to practice hearing due to an opposition expert witness statement that, on examination was seen to be highly biased and open to serious challenge, then there may be a case for the damaged party to take not only legal action against the dentist in question, but also regulatory action. The pendulum of justice just moved slightly back in our favour…but not by much. It would be very hard to prove bias where it existed and such a case would unlikely be funded by your indemnifier unless there was a strong case for it being in the interests of the indemnifier's members.

So what does an expert witness do

- Experts should give the facts as they see them and state the assumptions that form the basis of their evidence
- The facts should include matters that go against the expert's opinion where such exists
- The expert must state when an issue falls outside his/her expertise
- If s/he does not have the information needed to state an opinion, the expert should state so
- If the expert has to qualify an opinion, this should be stated
- If the expert's opinion changes following an exchange of reports, the expert should state this
- If the expert refers to documents such as guidance or court cases, this should be provided to the courts.
- Expert evidence is one of the only forms of opinion evidence that can be admissible as evidence of the facts.
- The expert has to be competent to give the evidence (so it would be a mistake for a GDP to be asked to give evidence on a multiple implant case unless s/he had enough experience). If the requisite experience is lacking, the expert WILL be found out, which can be a humiliating experience.
- An expert may be required to go to court/GDC hearing to give evidence
- The expert's evidence will only be admissible if the court feels it requires the evidence, which would invariably be the case in complex negligence cases
- The evidence must be reliable, and this can be difficult to ascertain when the evidence involves new techniques.
- And as already stated, the expert must be impartial

- The Expert is not allowed to comment on the "Ultimate Issue", that being, s/he is not allowed to state an opinion on whether the dentist is in fact negligent for example. S/he should limit his opinion to the facts presented.
- It is unlikely the court will appoint a single joint witness in complex cases like negligence
- The expert witness presents his report and evidence for the benefit of the court/GDC panel. The court is not obliged to accept the evidence presented.
- An expert's evidence, can be rejected by the party instructing them. They can, if they wish, seek further opinion from another expert.

Ultimately the expert witness may be called to give evidence in a court of law or before a GDC panel. They will present their evidence under instruction from their solicitor or barrister, and the opposing side will then have the opportunity to cross examine. This can be a stressful and adversarial process. Once cross examined, the legal team for the expert's side can then re-examine the expert witness to help clarify any issues that cropped up under cross examination.

Negligence References

1. **Bolam v Friern Hospital Management Committee [1957] 1 WLR 583** - http://www.bailii.org/
2. **Maynard Vs West Midlands RHA [1984] 1 WLR 634** - http://www.bailii.org/
3. **Sidaway v Board of Governors of the Bethlem Royal Hospital [1985]** - http://www.bailii.org/
4. **Bolitho v City and Hackney Health Authority [1997] 4 All ER 771 -** http://www.bailii.org/
5. **Brooks V Home office [1999]** - http://www.bailii.org/
6. **Bull V Devon AHA [1993] 4 Med LR 117** - http://www.bailii.org/
7. **Wilsher V Essex A.H.A. [1986] 3 All ER 801-** http://www.bailii.org/
8. **Montgomery v Lanarkshire Health Board [2013] CSIH** 3 - http://www.bailii.org/
9. **Rogers v Whitaker [1993] 4 Med. L.R. 79 -** http://www.bailii.org/
10. **Philippa White, Consent after Montgomery: What next for healthcare professionals? Clinical Risk 2016, Vol. 22 3337**
11. **GMC: Good Practice** - http://www.gmcuk.org/good_medical_practice_oct_1995.pdf_25416576.pdf
12. **Good Medical Practice and Consent: Patients and Doctors Making Decisions Together. GMC 2008** - http://www.gmc-uk.org/guidance/ethical_guidance/consent_guidance_index.asp
13. **Bonnington Castings v Wardlaw [1956] 1 All ER 615** - http://www.bailii.org/
14. **McGhee v N.C.B. [1972] 3 All ER** - http://www.bailii.org/

15. **Limitation act 1980** - https://www.legislation.gov.uk/ukpga/1980/

16. **E v English Province of Our Lady of Charity [2012] EWCA Civ 938** - http://www.bailii.org/
17. **Various Claimants v Catholic Child Welfare Society [2012] UKSC 56** - http://www.bailii.org/
18. **Woodland v Essex County Council** - http://www.bailii.org/
19. **Whetstone V MPS** - http://www.bailii.org/ew/cases/EWHC/QB/2014/1024.html
20. **http://www.the-dentist.co.uk/archive/article/3594/facts-and-fiction**
21. **Various Claimants v Barclays Bank PLC [2017] EWHC 1929 (QB)** - http://www.bailii.org/
22. **Civil procedure Rules (CPR)** - https://www.justice.gov.uk/courts/procedure-rules/civil/rules
23. **Jackson Reforms** - https://www.judiciary.gov.uk/wp-content/uploads/JCO/Documents/Reports/jackson-final-report-140110.pdf
24. **Conditional Fees Agreements Regulations (1995)** - http://www.legislation.gov.uk/uksi/2000/692/contents/made
25. **Pre-Action Protocol** - http://www.justice.gov.uk/courts/procedure-rules/civil/rules/pd_pre-action_conduct
26. **Alternative Dispute Resolution** - http://www.justice.gov.uk/courts/procedure-rules/civil/rules/pd_pre-action_conduct#8.1
27. **Civil Evidence Act 1995** - http://www.legislation.gov.uk/ukpga/1995/38/contents

28. **jones v kaney** - https://en.wikipedia.org/wiki/Jones_v_Kaney
29. **Part 35 Civil procedure rules** - https://www.justice.gov.uk/courts/procedure-rules/civil/rules/part35/pd_part35 **&** https://www.justice.gov.uk/courts/procedure-rules/civil/rules/part35

Record keeping

Clinical records are essential to keep track of your care for your patients. They tell you where you have been, where you are, and where you are going. You have all experienced that little heart sink where you have a patient booked in and, for one reason or another, you didn't mark down what you were actually supposed to be doing.

"So as to check that I have your full understanding, please relay back to me what we intended to do today"... I actually heard a dentist say that once instead of just being honest. It didn't work.

However, they also serve another purpose, a medico legal purpose. Notes of old were usually of such poor standard as to be useless in today's clinical negligence cases. Gone are the days where you could get away with Exam, S/P TC. The GDC expect you to follow the guidance laid out for record keeping. Unfortunately, the guidance is severely lacking. For example

- **There is no official guidance on what to record for restorative dentistry**
- **There is no official guidance on what to record for prosthetic dentistry**
- **There is no official guidance on what to record for Oral Surgery**

Believe me, I've looked. There is however guidance on record keeping in examination (from FGDP via their open standards), for RCT's (via the European society of endodontology)[1] and for Perio (from the British Society of Periodontology)[2], and my interpretation of that can be found in **Appendix 7.**

The dental records belong to the dental practice, but patients are allowed to obtain copies as already discussed. The ISO standard, **ISO 15489-1:2016 Information and documentation - Records management 8**[3] defines a record as

"information created, received, and maintained as evidence and information by an organisation or person, in pursuance of legal obligations or in the transaction of business".

But what exactly do we mean by dental records:

- **Medical history**
- **Handwritten or computerised notes of all treatment**
- **Radiographs and their associated written reports**
- **Referral letters with responses**
- **Copies of written treatment plans**
- **FP17's**
- **Patient communications and complaints (including emails and texts)**
- **Full patient details (Address etc.)**
- **Study models, photographs, stents etc.**
- **Laboratory instruction sheets**
- **Signed consent forms**
- **Videos and audio recordings**

The standard of what you are expected to record is now quite high. It is also important to remember that records don't just relate to patients, but also to staff too. Watch out for that when we talk about the CQC guidance to record keeping in a moment.

Your regulatory obligation

GDC

I am sure you aren't surprised to learn that the GDC have issued guidance on this topic.

4.1 You must make and keep contemporaneous, complete and accurate patient records

Guidance

4.1.1 You must make and keep complete and accurate patient records, including an up-to-date medical history, each time that you treat patients. Radiographs, consent forms, photographs, models, audio or visual recordings of consultations, laboratory prescriptions, statements of conformity and referral letters all form part of patients records where they are available.
Comment - You need an up to date medical history every time you treat the patient. The standards don't state whether this can be done verbally, or if it has to be a signed sheet. It does however strongly imply you have to record and ask them about their medical history every time you treat them. So that's every visit, even if the visits are a day apart. This is a must

4.1.2 You should record as much detail as possible about the discussions you have with your patients, including evidence that valid consent has been obtained. You should also include details of any particular patient's treatment needs where appropriate.
Comment - Basically everything you say to the patient regarding their treatment should be recorded

4.1.3 You must understand and meet your responsibilities in relation to patient information in line with current legislation. You must follow appropriate national advice on retaining, storing and disposing of patient records.

4.1.4 You must ensure that all documentation that records your work, including patient records, is clear, legible, accurate, and can be readily understood by others. You must also record the name or initials of the treating clinician. Comment - You must record who the treating clinician is. Initials are acceptable. Your notes have to be legible. If you write in a spider scrawl, you now breach GDC standards

4.1.5 If you need to make any amendments to a patient's records you must make sure that the changes are clearly marked up and dated. **Comment** - one of the things the GDC hate more than anything is notes that have been changed after the fact. If you do this, you must write that these notes are additional and why they were written at a later date. To do otherwise makes it look like you were trying to protect yourself after the fact which will most likely add a dishonesty charge onto whatever the GDC want to throw at you.

4.1.6 If you refer a patient to another dental professional or other health professional, you must make an accurate record of this referral in the patient's notes and include a written prescription when necessary.

The CQC

The CQC cover record keeping in **Regulation 17: Good Governance**[4]

17(2)(c) maintain securely an accurate, complete and contemporaneous record in respect of each service user, including a record of the care and treatment provided to the service user and of decisions taken in relation to the care and treatment provided;

- *Records relating to service users' care and treatment are created/amended, stored and destroyed in accordance with current legislation and guidance: -Records are complete, legible, accurate and every effort must be made to ensure records are updated without any delays e.g. results of diagnostic test, correspondence etc., should be added as soon as possible.*
- *Records must be kept secure at all times and only accessed, amended, or destroyed by persons authorised to do so.*
- *Individual service user records are fit for purpose and can be accessed by authorised persons as required in order to deliver their care and treatment in a manner which meets their needs and keeps them safe.*
- *Individual service records should accurately record all decisions taken in relation to care and treatment and may reference to discussions with service users/relevant persons, consent records, advanced decisions to refuse treatment, etc.*
- *Decisions taken on behalf of a service user due to lack of capacity must be recorded and provide evidence that these have been taken in accordance with the requirements of the Mental Capacity Act 2005 or where relevant the Mental Health Act 1983, and their associated Codes of Practice.*
    - *Information in all formats is managed in accordance with current legislation and guidance.*
    - *Systems and processes support service users' confidentiality and do not contravene the Data Protection Act 1998.*

17(2)(d) maintain securely such other records as are necessary to be kept in relation to–
(i) persons employed in the carrying on of the regulated activity, and
(ii) the management of the regulated activity;

- *Records relating to persons employed and the management of regulated activities are created/ amended, stored and destroyed in accordance with current legislation and guidance.*

- ***Records relating to persons employed should include information relevant to their being employed in the role including information relating to the requirements under Regulations 5 (Fit and proper person (directors)) and Regulation 19 (Fit and proper persons employed).***
- ***Records relating to the management of regulated activities mean anything relevant to the design and delivery of care and treatment, and may include governance arrangements such as policies and procedures, service/maintenance records, audits and reviews, purchasing, action plans in response to risks/incidents, etc.***
- ***Records are complete, legible, indelible, accurate and up to date, with no undue delays in adding/ filing information, insofar as is reasonably practicable. Information must not be unduly delayed from being added to/filed in records.***
- ***Records must be kept secure at all times and only accessed, amended or destroyed by authorised persons.***
    - ***Information in all formats is managed in accordance with current legislation and guidance.***

Systems and processes support service users' confidentiality and do not contravene the Data Protection Act 1998

Also remember that the regulators cross over. So the GDC will expect you to comply with anything the CQC states. The GDC give some useful advice on this in the mythbuster series[5]. It would appear that the CQC expect you to follow FGDP, GDC and IRMER 2000 regulations/guidance. When they inspect, they will expect to see the following in the clinical notes:

- Patient identification data
- Medical history
- Disease risk assessment
- Dental history
- Clinical examination details
- Radiographic examination (if applicable)

- Diagnosis (where appropriate)
- Treatment plan
- Reference to consent
- Progress notes
- Periodontal screening tools including BPE
- Specific soft tissue examinations
- Dental X-rays/radiographs(where appropriate)
- Screening methods for dental decay
- Details of the treatment carried out
- Details of any products supplied or administered to a patient including the manufacturer and batch number used
- Details of procedure and whether any post-operative instructions were given.
- If antibiotics or other drugs are prescribed then justification for the prescription type, dose and duration - there appears to be no guidance on how one records a justification
- If treatment was carried out using injected local anaesthetic, there should be a record of the type of drug, the route of administration, the volume used and the manufacturer. Batch number and expiry date can be recorded elsewhere in the practice as part of practice wide policy on the storage of medicines. I have struggled to find the actual legislation governing these specific requirements
- Details of the different treatment options and the risks and benefits
- Written consent forms for some treatments
- Written treatment plans detailing individual treatments and their costs; making it clear what is being proposed as NHS treatment and what as private treatment
- Relevant NHS paperwork

- Evidence that oral health and dietary advice has been given as per the DOH toolkit 'Delivering better oral health- an evidence based toolkit for prevention'

The NHS

Record keeping does not just cover how to fill out records. It also covers their retention and disposal. As we saw in the confidentiality section, it's important that they are securely held in a way that only those who should view them get to see them. The document "**Records Management Code of Practice**"[6] outlines much of what you need to know. It would be safe to say that private practitioners would be wise to follow the same principles set out by the NHS, because much of it is created by legislation. Here is what the NHS Dental Contract presently states:

Part 5

Patient records

32.—(1) The contractor shall ensure that a full, accurate and contemporaneous record is kept in the patient record in respect of the care and treatment given to each patient under the contract, including treatment given to a patient who is referred to the contractor. **Comment** - you will notice there is no definition in the contract of what contemporaneous means

(2) The patient record may be kept in electronic form.

(3) The patient record shall include details of any private services (to the extent that they are provided with services under the contract) and shall be kept with—

(a) a copy of any treatment plan or referral treatment plan given to the patient pursuant to paragraph 2 of Schedule 1 (referral services) or paragraph 7 of this Schedule;

(b) all radiographs, photographs and study casts taken or obtained by it as part of the services provided to that patient;
(c) where an orthodontic course of treatment has been provided to a patient, a copy of the orthodontic treatment plan;
(d) where information is to be submitted to the Primary Care Trust in accordance with paragraph 38 and that information is submitted electronically—

(i) the written declaration form in respect of exemption under paragraph 1(1) of Schedule 12ZA to the Act duly made and completed in accordance regulations made under section 79 of, and paragraph 7(a) to, Schedule 12ZA to that Act; and

(ii) a note of the evidence in support of that declaration; and

(e) the statement concerning any custom-made devices provided by any person as a consequence of regulation 15 of the Medical Devices Regulations 2002(a) (procedures for custom-made devices) in respect of services being provided to that patient. **Comment** - regulation 15 of the Medical Devices Regulations 2002[7] will be discussed shortly.

(4) The patient record and the items referred to in sub-paragraph (3) shall be retained for a period of 2 years beginning with—

(a) the date on which—

(i) a course of treatment or orthodontic course of treatment is terminated; or

(ii) a course of treatment or an orthodontic course of treatment is completed; or

(b) in respect of courses of treatment or orthodontic courses of treatment not falling within paragraph

> ***(a)(i) or (ii) the date by which no more services can be provided as part of that course of treatment or orthodontic course of treatment by virtue of paragraph 5(4)(b) of Schedule 1 (orthodontic course of treatment) or paragraph 6(4)(b) of this Schedule.***

(5) Nothing in this paragraph shall affect any property right which the contractor may have in relation to the records, radiographs, photographs and study models referred to in this paragraph.

So regarding that bit from the medical devices regulations, you need to pay attention to this, because it applies to private treatment as well. We might as well take a moment and talk about that now.

Custom medical devices

I'm going to take you down a rabbit hole. You won't like where we come out, but it's important we go there. It's these little things that seem almost designed to trip you up. If it wasn't important, the GDC wouldn't have written a two-page document on the matter. Both the GDC and legislation cover this. The GDC mention it in their 2013 "**Guidance on commissioning and manufacturing dental appliances**"[8] which is actually somewhat difficult to find on the GDC website. Use Dr Google. It makes several points:

Registrants providing patients with a dental appliance

The Medical Devices Directive 93/42/EC requires that the statement of manufacture is available to the patient for whom the dental appliance is made. The patient can request this at any time during the lifetime of the appliance. You must inform patients of the existence of the statement and offer them a copy. You must record whether or not they choose to take a copy of it. If the patient does not choose to take a copy of the statement, you must keep the statement for the lifetime of the device in case it is requested at a later date.

So what does the Medical Devices Directive say? Procedures for custom-made general medical devices:

15. No person shall supply a custom-made device (if that supply is also a placing on the market, or if that supply is of a custom-made device that has been placed on the market) unless its manufacturer or his authorised representative—

> ***(a)has drawn up a statement containing the information required by Sections 1, 2 and 2.1 of Annex VIII;***
>
> ***(b)has undertaken to keep available for the Secretary of State documentation allowing an understanding of the design, manufacture and performances of the device, including the expected performances, so as to allow assessment of conformity of the device with the requirements of Directive 93/42; and***
>
> ***(c)takes all necessary measures to ensure that the manufacturing process ensures that each device manufactured according to that process conforms to the documentation referred to in the first paragraph of Section 3.1 of Annex VIII; and***
>
> ***(d)keeps available for the Secretary of State, for a minimum period of five years, the information contained in the***

statement referred to in paragraph (a) and in the undertaking referred to in paragraph (b).

Now what the bloody hell does that all mean? Well believe it or not, the GDC help you here. If we go back to their Guidance on commissioning and manufacturing dental appliances:

Registrants who manufacture dental appliances mainly outside of the mouth (for example- fixed bridges, bleaching trays, crowns, splints, retainers, etc.) If you make a dental appliance, whether you are a dental technician, dentist, or any other registrant, you must understand and comply with your legal responsibilities as "manufacturer" under the Medical Devices Directive 93/42/EC. This includes the legal requirement to register with the Medicines and Healthcare Products Regulatory Agency (MHRA). You must provide a statement of manufacture which gives the following information when dispatching a dental appliance:

- ***the name and address of the manufacturer, and if outside the EEA their authorised representative,***
- ***data allowing identification of the device in question,***
- ***a statement that the device is a Custom-made Dental Appliance and intended for exclusive use by a particular patient, together with the name of the patient,***
- ***the name of the practitioner or other authorised person who made out the prescription and, where applicable, the name of the practice concerned,***
- ***the specific characteristics of the product as indicated by the prescription,***
- ***a statement that the device in question conforms to the essential requirements set out in Annex I of the Medical***

Devices Directive 93/42/EC and, where applicable, indicating which essential requirements have not been fully met, together with the grounds

But what exactly is a medical device. The interpretation of this comes from the **Medical Devices Regulations**:

"medical device" means an instrument, apparatus, appliance, material or other article, whether used alone or in combination, together with any software necessary for its proper application, which—

(a)is intended by the manufacturer to be used for human beings for the purpose of-

(i)diagnosis, prevention, monitoring, treatment or alleviation of disease,

(ii)diagnosis, monitoring, treatment, alleviation of or compensation for an injury or handicap,

(iii)investigation, replacement or modification of the anatomy or of a physiological process, or

(iv)control of conception; and

(b)does not achieve its principal intended action in or on the human body by pharmacological, immunological or metabolic means, even if it is assisted in its function by such means,

So a temporary crown is potentially a medical device because it is intended by the manufacturer (you) to be used for the purpose of treating disease. It could be argued that a temporary crown, veneer or bridge that is done as part of a purely cosmetic procedure would fall outside of this. But what about a chairside NTI-tss? What about a lucia jig. Those are definitely custom made appliances. My communication with the GDC and the **Medicines and healthcare products Regulatory Agency** (MHRA) all say that yes, these are medical devices and as such dentists making them need to be registered with the MHRA. More information can be obtained from the MHRA document - "**Custom made medical devices**"[9].

By the way, if you choose to go down this route (and please check with your indemnifier as I might be wrong on this) be prepared for the fact that getting registered is a bit like herding cats. In the dark. With both legs encased in concrete. Have fun.

Retention of records

There are strict rules over how long dental records should be retained (we will be highlighting on retention in a dental practice environment, not a hospital setting). The Data Protection Act states that "*Personal data shall not be kept for longer than is necessary for that purpose or those purposes*". When you think about it, this isn't actually very helpful. You have to keep the records for a certain period of time, but you can't keep them too long.

In a nutshell the advice on retention is as follows (this applies to both NHS and private records):

- **For adults, keep all records for a minimum of 11 years after the last entry.**
- **For children keep all records for a minimum of 11 years after the last entry or until they attain the age of 25 (whichever time period is longer).**

But where does this advice come from? It's all very good me saying that, but for all you know I could be plucking years out of the ether. Let's see if we can pin this down.

The document "**Records Management Code of Practice for Health and Social Care 2016**"[10] published by the Information Governance Alliance applies to NHS records, and includes patient records, records of staff and complaints in both digital and paper format. Said records must be held securely so as to limit access so that only those with the proper permissions can access them. Here are some of the juicy bits from this document:

- Staff clinical training records should be retained until 6 years after the staff member leaves or until they reach 75, whichever is the longer. I know the government are intent for us to work till a ripe old age but…
- Statutory and mandatory training records (Cross infection etc) should be retained for 10 years after training is complete
- For other training records, these should be kept for 6 years after training is complete

Another document, the 2011 NHS document "**Retention and Disposal of Records Policy and procedure**"[11] outlines the retention period expected for ALL documents (whilst this specifically only covers NHS practice, it would be reasonable to expect much of this to be applicable to private practice also). This list can be found in **Appendix 8**.

Just a small point, but do you ever communicate with NHS patients via email or social media? Ask yourselves if that becomes part of the clinical records. As stated in the records management code - "*This may not necessarily mean that the social media must be captured but rather the information of the activity through transcription or periodic storage.*"

Article 5 of GDPR states - "*kept in a form which permits identification of data subjects for no longer than is necessary for the purposes for which the personal data are processed; personal data may be stored for longer periods insofar as the personal data will be processed solely for archiving purposes in the public interest, scientific or historical research purposes or statistical purposes"*

Record disposal

The information on record disposal comes from a number of different sources. When you destroy records, it is advisable to do so using a certified destruction service who will invoice you so there is a record that the records have been destroyed in a proper fashion that meets an international standard. There are numerous pieces of guidance on this, but the recognised standard for record destruction can be found in the British Security Industry Association guide "**Information Destruction EN15713:2009 Guide**"[12] …it's a thrilling, rollercoaster of a read.

A few extra points…

LA batch numbers

A quick point on recording LA batch numbers. According to advice from DPL, they don't have to be recorded in your clinical records (although it might be easy enough to do so). It does seem however that some record needs to be made. This can be in your stock records or through some other means.

Indemnifier advice

There is also some advice from the dental indemnifiers who are tasked with defending dental professionals against litigious and regulatory claims. Good record keeping is essential for fighting claims of litigation and it therefor makes sense for those who indemnify dental professionals to give advice regarding the keeping of records. The Dental Defence Union (DDU), in their guide **Dental Records**[13] state that good records should ‘follow the four C’s, Contemporaneous, Clear, Concise and Complete' (p.31). Specifically, they advised that all aspects of a patient’s visit should be recorded. This includes:

- presenting complaints
- histories (medical, dental and social)
- dental charting
- findings on examination, including negative findings
- diagnosis
- discussions about treatment options and risks
- agreed treatment plan and record of consent to treatment
- treatment given
- mishaps and complications
- all reports should be recorded and complete

Whilst useful, this advice is somewhat vague in my opinion. Dental Protection Limited (DPL) also give advice in one of their Risk Management Modules. On the aspect of recording treatment in this publication, we get some detail on what should be included in the clinical notes. According to DPL, the treatment should specify the date, the teeth treated, materials used and clinical findings of the treatment. There should be a recording of signs and symptoms as well as negative findings. There should be a record of all discussions, consent and any investigations with their results.

Record Keeping References

1. **European society of endodontology** - http://onlinelibrary.wiley.com/doi/10.1111/j.1365-2591.2006.01180.x/pdf
2. **BSP Young practitioners guide** - https://www.bsperio.org.uk/publications/good_practitioners_guide_2016.pdf?v=3
3. **ISO 15489-1:2016 Information and documentation - Records management 8** - https://www.bsperio.org.uk/publications/good_practitioners_guide_2016.pdf?v=3
4. **Regulation 17: Good Governance** - http://www.cqc.org.uk/sites/default/files/20150324_guidance_providers_meeting_regulations_01.pdf
5. **CQC mythbusters** - http://www.cqc.org.uk/guidance-providers/dentists/dental-mythbuster-8-dental-care-records
6. **DOH: Records Management Code of Practice** - https://www.gov.uk/government/publications/records-management-code-of-practice-for-health-and-social-care
7. **Medical Devices Regulations 2002** - http://www.legislation.gov.uk/uksi/2002/618/contents/made
8. **GDC: Guidance on commissioning and manufacturing dental appliances** - google lol
9. **MHRA: Custom made medical devices** - https://www.gov.uk/government/uploads/system/uploads/attachment_data/file/398428/Custom_made_devices.pdf
10. **Records Management Code of Practice for Health and Social Care 2016** - https://digital.nhs.uk/article/1202/Records-Management-Code-of-Practice-for-Health-and-Social-Care-2016

11. **Retention and Disposal of Records Policy and procedure** - http://www.heartofengland.nhs.uk/wp-content/uploads /Attachment-7-08-11.pdf
12. **Information Destruction EN15713:2009 Guide** - https://www.bsia.co.uk/Portals/4/Publications/form_204_id_en15713.pdf
13. **DDU: Dental Records** - https://www.theddu.com/guidance-and-advice/guides/dental-records/keeping-good-records

The Rest

So as with anything like this, there will always be things left out that need to be mentioned. This chapter will deal with such issues and will mainly be opinion based.

Audit

As you would expect, audit is important to the CQC, specifically **Regulations 12, 15 and 17**. There are several types of audit that are mandatory:

- Infection prevention and control
- X-rays
- Accessibility - Needed to comply with the Equality Act 2010[1]

You are also strongly advised to do audit in (just an example, not a definitive list):

- Patient Satisfaction and patient waiting times
- Communication quality and delivery of services from your dental laboratory
- Staff satisfaction
- Record keeping
- Patient non attendance
- Referrals

Further advice on audit can be found in the Royal College of Surgeons free publication "**Methodologies for Clinical Audit in Dentistry**"[2]

Cross Infection

You will be expected to follow the following

- **HTM 01-05**[3] (well obviously)
- **The Health and Social Care Act 2008: Code of Practice on the prevention and control of infections and related guidance**[4]. This also covers the validation of decontamination equipment (also see the **Pressure Systems Safety Regulations 2000**[5])

As stated you will need to do a cross infection audit every six months (keep an eye on this, because they do change it. The audit tool by the **Infection Prevention Society** can presently be found on Gov.uk[6]

Equality Act 2010[7]

You would be wrong to think this only applies to patients. It applies to staff also, protecting those with disabilities as well as those who had disabilities in the past. Let's look and see what the Act actually states (it's quite a large piece of legislation so a summary is the best I can offer here). The Equality Act 2010 replaced the Equal Pay Act 1970, Sex Discrimination Act 1975, Race Relations Act 1976, Disability Discrimination Act 1995, Employment Equality (Religion or Belief) Regulations 2003, Employment Equality (Sexual Orientation) Regulations 2003 and the Employment Equality (Age) Regulations 2006. See, I told you it was big.

This basically revolves around taking reasonable action to achieve equality of access for those with disabilities (both physical and mental), as well as giving protection (and thus preventing discrimination) based on age, disability, gender reassignment, marriage and civil partnership, pregnancy and maternity, race, religion or belief, sex and sexual orientation. You will remember that this is highlighted in GDC standard 1.6.1.

You, as a primary health care provider, have a duty to determine how your business meets the needs of service users (by doing an accessibility audit) as well as determining what "reasonable adjustments" need to be made to meet any deficiencies. What do they mean by reasonable? Well generally, the easier the adjustment is to make, the more likely you will have been expected to make it. So if you work out of an old property, some would say it isn't reasonable to expect you to undergo an extension to put in a disabled toilet, but attaching some grab bars to the walls of the existing toilet as well as some kind of panic alarm would be very reasonable. If you feel an adjustment is needed, you should ask yourself (for example):

- **Is the adjustment feasible and how much disruption would it cause?**
- **Is the adjustment affective?**
- **Will it be worth the time and effort to make the adjustment, as well as the cost implications?**
- **What impact do disabled service users face if the adjustment wasn't made?**
- **What costs have you already been subjected to in making adjustments and can those costs be passed on to all service users?**

The way to do this is via an access audit, which may mean bringing in an external consultant. If you decide not to make adjustments, you must be able to justify it. Of course, you should already be complying with this act so this is perhaps of historic interest only. But as already stated, the Act covers staff as well as patients. This is covered by part 39 of the Act

39 Employees and applicants

(1) An employer (A) must not discriminate against a person (B)—

(a)in the arrangements A makes for deciding to whom to offer employment;

(b)as to the terms on which A offers B employment;

(c)by not offering B employment.

(2) An employer (A) must not discriminate against an employee of A's (B)—

(a)as to B's terms of employment;

(b)in the way A affords B access, or by not affording B access, to opportunities for promotion, transfer or training or for receiving any other benefit, facility or service;

(c)by dismissing B;

(d)by subjecting B to any other detriment.

(3) An employer (A) must not victimise a person (B)—

(a)in the arrangements A makes for deciding to whom to offer employment;

(b)as to the terms on which A offers B employment;

(c)by not offering B employment.

(4) An employer (A) must not victimise an employee of A's (B)—

(a)as to B's terms of employment;

(b)in the way A affords B access, or by not affording B access, to opportunities for promotion, transfer or training or for any other benefit, facility or service;

(c)by dismissing B;

(d)by subjecting B to any other detriment.

(5) A duty to make reasonable adjustments applies to an employer.

(6) Subsection (1)(b), so far as relating to sex or pregnancy and maternity, does not apply to a term that relates to pay—

(a)unless, were B to accept the offer, an equality clause or rule would have effect in relation to the term, or

(b)if paragraph (a) does not apply, except in so far as making an offer on terms including that term amounts to a contravention of subsection (1)(b) by virtue of section 13, 14 or 18.

(7) In subsections (2)(c) and (4)(c), the reference to dismissing B includes a reference to the termination of B's employment—

(a)by the expiry of a period (including a period expiring by reference to an event or circumstance);

(b)by an act of B's (including giving notice) in circumstances such that B is entitled, because of A's conduct, to terminate the employment without notice.

(8) Subsection (7)(a) does not apply if, immediately after the termination, the employment is renewed on the same terms.

40 Employees and applicants: harassment

(9) An employer (A) must not, in relation to employment by A, harass a person (B)—

(a)who is an employee of A's;

(b)who has applied to A for employment.

Basically, you as an employer can't:

- Treat a job applicant or employee less favourably than others because of disability. Positive discrimination in favour of a disabled job applicant or employee is allegedly allowed. Surely the best person for the position should get the job?
- Treat a job applicant or employee unfavourably because of something arising because of disability without good justification.
- Discriminate by applying a provision or practice that penalises job applicants or employees with a disability without good
  reason.

- Fail to make reasonable adjustments where a disabled job applicant or employee is put at a substantial disadvantage.
- Harass someone based on their disability.
- Victimise someone because they intend to make a disability discrimination complaint under the Equality Act 2010.
- Ask job applicants pre-employment health questions other than for a prescribed reason.

Employment law is too complex to be fully covered in this book. We strongly advise you employ an external law firm to make sure you are compliant with all aspects of employment law. There are several now offering monthly retainer plans.

GDC Standards

I have already talked a lot on this topic, but there are a few further things I want you to think about. I'm not going to talk about standards I have already covered or that I feel need no further comment:

1.1.1 You must discuss treatment options with patients and listen carefully to what they say. Give them the opportunity to have a discussion and to ask questions - **Comment**: Can you do this in a 5-minute check-up?

1.2 You must treat every patient with dignity and respect at all times - **Comment**: This is why I say dentists should only treat patients that they like and who like them. Because if you are Hungry, Angry, running late, stressed or tired, this will all have an impact on your communication. Are you allowed to have human frailties under GDC standards?

1.2.4 You should manage patients' dental pain and anxiety appropriately. - **Comment**: What about hot pulps?

1.3 You <u>must</u> be honest and act with integrity

1.3.1 You <u>must</u> justify the trust that patients, the public and your colleagues place in you by always acting honestly and fairly in your dealings with them. This applies to any business or education activities in which you are involved as well as to your professional dealings. - **Comment**: So can you continue to help promote the mantra that private care is the same as NHS care? Because it clearly isn't.

1.3.3 You <u>must</u> make sure that any advertising, promotional material or other information that you produce is accurate and not misleading, and complies with the GDC's guidance on ethical advertising - **Comment**: - laser whitening? Same day teeth? Holistic amalgam removal?

1.4 You <u>must</u> take a holistic and preventative approach to patient care which is appropriate to the individual patient

1.4.2 You <u>must</u> provide patients with treatment that is in their best interests, providing appropriate oral health advice and following clinical guidelines relevant to their situation. You may need to balance their oral health needs with their desired outcomes. If their desired outcome is not achievable or is not in the best interests of their oral health, you must explain the risks, benefits and likely outcomes to help them to make a decision - **Comment**: where is the national guidance? There is some from Scotland but nothing for England as far as I know, so everyone will be doing things differently. The DOH document "Delivering Oral health"[8] doesn't really go into the how, rather it concentrates on the what

1.6.1 You <u>must</u> not discriminate against patients on the grounds of:

- ***Age,***

- ***Disability,***
- ***Gender reassignment,***
- ***Marriage and civil partnership***
- ***Pregnancy and maternity, Race,***
- ***Religion or belief,***
- ***Sex,***
- ***Sexual orientation.***

You must also ensure that you do not discriminate against patients or groups of patients for any other reasons such as nationality, special needs, health, lifestyle or any other consideration. - **Comment**: Also, one man's discrimination is another man's common sense. "He refused to see me and discriminated against me because I turned up 30 minutes late".

1.7 You must put patients' interests before your own or those of any colleague, business or organisation - **Comment**: This seems to imply that the interests of all your patients as a whole is the priority. How does this affect individual patients? If I'm spending 3 hours doing high class molar endo in a busy NHS practice with high demand, some would argue this is detrimental to your patient base on the whole because you have less time to see them. It's vague and open to interpretation by both sides.

1.7.1 You must always put your patients' interests before any financial, personal or other gain. - **Comment**: Is this even reasonable? Think about it. An impossible standard to meet? It is after all in the patient's best interests to receive all their treatment for free. It is in the patient's best interest for you to treat them when it is convenient for them, even if that is at the weekend.

1.7.2 If you work in a practice that provides both NHS (or equivalent health service) and private treatment (a mixed practice), you must make clear to your patients which treatments can be provided under the NHS (or equivalent health service) and which can only be provided on a private basis. - **Comment**: so where is the list of treatments that are available on the NHS. The GDC will refuse your request for such a list and will say it is for you to find this information out.

1.7.6 When you are referring patients to another member of the dental team, you must make sure that the referral is made in the patients' best interests rather than for your own, or another team member's, financial gain or benefit. - **Comment** single patient or all your patients? It is in the private endodontist's financial interests to have patients referred to him/her.

1.7.7 If you believe that patients might be at risk because of your health, behaviour or professional performance or that of a colleague, or because of any aspect of the clinical environment, you must take prompt and appropriate action. - **Comment**: So if you are burnt out, stressed, suffering illness that impacts the job, the GDC are telling you here to do something about it. "But I can't take time off"....you don't have a choice. In a way, the GDC are trying to look out for your wellbeing here, they could just make that more obvious. The time you think you can't take time off is exactly the time you should in a lot of cases

1.7.8 In rare circumstances, the trust between you and a patient may break down, and you may find it necessary to end the professional relationship. You should not stop providing a service to a patient solely because of a complaint the patient has made about you or your team. Before you end a professional relationship with a patient, you must be satisfied that your decision is fair and you must be able to justify your decision. You should write to the patient to tell them your decision and your reasons for it. You should take steps to ensure that arrangements are made promptly for the continuing care of the patient. - **Comment**: there you go, the GDC just told you what you need to do to get rid of a patient.

1.9 You must find out about laws and regulations that affect your work and follow them

1.9.1 You <u>must</u> find out about, and follow, laws and regulations affecting your work. This includes, but is not limited to, those relating to: data protection; employment; human rights and equality, registration with other regulatory bodies. - **<u>Comment</u>**: Perhaps this is why you are reading this book lol

2.1 You <u>must</u> communicate effectively with patients – listen to them, give them time to consider information and take their individual views and communication needs into account - **<u>Comment</u>**: Communication is key, because it is how you build trust and rapport. But what happens when the patient doesn't speak English? The available translation services are sub optimal, and using relatives to convey information has its drawbacks

2.2 You <u>must</u> recognise and promote patients' rights to and responsibilities for making decisions about their health priorities and care

2.2.1 You <u>must</u> listen to patients and communicate effectively with them at a level they can understand. Before treatment starts you must:

- ***explain the options (including those of delaying treatment or doing nothing) with the risks and benefits of each; and*** **<u>Comment</u>**: Give and record every option that you think is viable for treatment, including the option of no treatment. This all has to be recorded in the notes.
- ***give full information on the treatment you propose and the possible costs. 2.2.2 You should encourage patients to ask questions about their options or any aspect of their treatment.*** -**<u>Comment</u>**: The standard states you have to give "full information" but there is no definition. Does this mean we have to go down the American model of giving written risk sheets that go so far as to say there is a theoretical risk of death with LA? (no is the answer by the way). I think, as this is a must, the GDC need to specify what information they

want provided to the patient. But they don't, they leave it to us

- ***2.2.3 You <u>must</u> give full and honest answers to any questions patients have about their options or treatment.*** - **<u>Comment</u>**: And yet, if you truly believe amalgam is a dangerous material to use (as an example) you can be criticised for expressing your opinion if your information is delivered in a manner that a bureaucrat might object to.
- ***2.4 You must give patients clear information about costs***
- ***2.4.1 You <u>must</u> make sure that a simple price list is clearly displayed in your reception or waiting area. This <u>should</u> include a list of basic items including a consultation, a single-surface filling, an extraction, radiographs (bitewing or pan-oral) and treatment provided by the hygienist. For items which may vary in cost, a 'from — to' price range can be shown.*** - **<u>Comment</u>**: This doesn't take into account that you can't give a price for many treatments without first examining a patient.
- ***2.4.3 You <u>should</u> tell your patients whether treatment is guaranteed, under what circumstances and for how long. You should make clear any circumstances under which treatment is not guaranteed (for example, a lack of care on their part which leads to recurring problems).*** - **<u>Comment</u>**: If you guarantee treatment, you have to tell them the terms and conditions of that guarantee. By the way, if you give any kind of guarantee for private treatment you will breach contract law if the patient feels that guarantee has not been met. So perhaps don't do that

A few further points specific to Principle 2:

- If you want to work here, make sure you are fluent in English. One of the biggest causes of complaints is a lack of communication, and if you cannot communicate with the patient in a way they understand, you just breached the GDC standard
- Record everything and I mean everything regarding consent
- Formulate a practice policy on what information needs to be given to a patient, and give said information to them in writing
- Record all discussion and the options given to patients
- Introduce yourself and your staff
- Give FP17DC's or equivalent for all treatment. Private would probably be better with a bespoke treatment plan
- Have your practice details on everything, including the building
- Consider name badges or even practice photos of staff in reception
- Price lists in reception, website and on literature
- Don't give a guarantee unless you can back it up. And if you do give a guarantee put it in writing with strict T&C's

Let's carry on

4.5 You <u>must</u> keep patients' information secure at all times, whether your records are held on paper or electronically

4.5.1 You <u>must</u> make sure that patients' information is not revealed accidentally and that no-one has unauthorised access to it by storing it securely at all times. You <u>must</u> not leave records where they can be seen by other patients, unauthorised staff or members or the public. - **<u>Comment</u>**: Only those entitled to the records should be able to see them.

You must not leave records where they can be seen by members of the public. So if you are taking notes home and your car is stolen or broken into….

4.5.2 If you are sending confidential information, you should use a secure method. If you are sending or storing confidential information electronically, you should ensure that it is encrypted. - **Comment**: So the emailed referral letter to the Max Fax dept for an emergency appointment is right out unless both ends use encrypted email. And this raises the interesting question of whether you can send a fax. You don't know where that fax machine is in the department you are contacting.

4.5.3 If clinical records are computerised, you should make back-up copies of clinical records, radiographs and other images. - **Comment**: but if the backups are in the cloud you may be in breach. Many of the cloud providers, despite the assertions of security, are hackable and thus not secure. Just ask Jennifer Lawrence.

6.1 You must work effectively with your colleagues and contribute to good teamwork

6.1.2 You must treat colleagues fairly and with respect, in all situations and all forms of interaction and communication. You must not bully, harass, or unfairly discriminate against them. - **Comment**: We all know dentists who have a short fuse, who treat their staff like crap and who are even a bit lecherous. Act like that and it's a GDC matter. You must not bully, harass, or unfairly discriminate against people. I support this 100%

6.1.3 You must treat colleagues fairly in all financial transactions. - **Comment**: define fair. It's open to interpretation. Does this mean if you pay your lab late it become a matter for the GDC? Potentially yes. How's about the retention of fees when an associate moves practice?

6.1.6 As a registered dental professional, you could be held responsible for the actions of any member of your team who

does not have to register with the GDC (for example, receptionists, practice managers or laboratory assistants). You <u>should</u> ensure that they are appropriately trained and competent. - **<u>Comment</u>**: The GDC hold you vociferously liable for the actions of none GDC registered staff. However, the GDC don't say this to you as a boss, they state this to ALL GDC registrants. So if the cleaner isn't doing his/her job, could the whole team be held liable?

6.2 You <u>must</u> be appropriately supported when treating patients

6.2.1 You <u>must</u> not provide treatment if you feel that the circumstances make it unsafe for patients. - **<u>Comment</u>**: So there was a thread on Facebook about a dental corporate. Repeatedly associates were saying that pieces of equipment hadn't been fixed, how materials hadn't been ordered etc. etc. Are some corporates creating an environment where every GDC registered individual working in these practices are in breach of the GDC standards?

6.2.2 You <u>should</u> work with another appropriately trained member of the dental team at all times when treating patients in a dental setting. The only circumstances in which this does not apply are when:

- ***treating patients in an out of hours emergency,***
- ***providing treatment as part of a public health programme, or***
- ***there are exceptional circumstances.***

'Exceptional circumstances' are unavoidable circumstances which are not routine and could not have been foreseen. Absences due to leave or training are not exceptional circumstances. - **<u>Comment</u>**: Exceptional circumstances seems to include staff sickness. So if your nurse calls in sick you have to weigh up the risk/benefit of treating without a chaperone. By the way, if you are a hygienist and you don't work with a nurse, YOU breach the Standard. Strange though because my doctor is happy to see and examine me without a chaperone present? From a CQC point of view, if you are working single handed for whatever reason, you will be expected to have performed a risk assessment which needs to take into account how you would deal with a medical emergency…that's assuming you have time to see any patients what with all the paperwork ;)

6.2.6 Medical emergencies can happen at any time. You must make sure that there is at least one other person available within the working environment to deal with medical emergencies when you are treating patients. In exceptional circumstances the second person could be a receptionist or a person accompanying the patient. - **Comment**: so in an out of hours scenario whilst you don't need a chaperone, you still need another suitable member of staff in the building.

6.3 You must delegate and refer appropriately and effectively

6.3.1 You can delegate the responsibility for a task but not the accountability. This means that, although you can ask someone to carry out a task for you, you could still be held accountable if something goes wrong. You should only delegate or refer to another member of the team if you are confident that they have been trained and are both competent and indemnified to do what you are asking. For more information, see the 'Scope of Practice' document. - **Comment**: Look at the language there, "held accountable".

6.3.3 You should refer patients on if the treatment required is outside your scope of practice or competence. You should be clear about the procedure for doing this. - **Comment**: Notice that this is a should, not a must. The only way you can become competent at something is to first do something that you are not overly competent doing, and much of this isn't given to you by your dental school training. But if you leave dental school without the requisite level of competence, should the GDC not address this… because they set and approve the university curriculum?

6.4 You must only accept a referral or delegation if you are trained and competent to carry out the treatment and you believe that what you are being asked to do is appropriate for the patient

6.4.2 If you do not think that what you have been asked to do is appropriate, you should discuss this with the colleague who asked you to do it. You should only go ahead if you are satisfied that what you have been asked to do is appropriate. If you are not sure, you should seek advice from your professional association or defence organisation. - **Comment**: Have you ever sent off a referral, say for a wisdom tooth, only for the referring dentist to decline because s/he didn't agree? Did they contact you? Or did they just bat the patient back to you?

6.6 You must demonstrate effective management and leadership skills if you manage a team

6.6.5 You must encourage, support and facilitate the continuing professional development (CPD) of your dental team. - **Comment**: That's a MUST. If a DCP doesn't do her required CPD, you risk being held at fault as well as them

6.6.6 Medical emergencies can happen at any time in a dental practice. You must make sure that:

- ***there are arrangements for at least two people to be available within the working environment to deal with medical emergencies when treatment is planned to take place;***
- ***all members of staff, including those not registered with the GDC, know their role if there is a medical emergency; and***
- ***all members of staff who might be involved in dealing with a medical emergency are trained and prepared to do so at any time, and practise together regularly in a simulated emergency so they know exactly what to do.*** - **Comment**: During normal surgery hours, at least two team members trained in medical emergencies MUST be present. - All members of staff MUST have a designated role in the case of medical emergencies, and they MUST know their role

6.6.7 You should ensure your team has:

- ***good leadership;***
- ***clear, shared aims; and***
- ***an understanding of their roles and responsibilities.*** - **Comment**: You should ensure your team has good leadership. So what if you are the practice owner and you are a little Hitler how do you think this is going to go?

6.6.10 You should display information about the members of your team (including their registration number where appropriate), in an area where it can be easily seen by patients. - **Comment**: You need to display your staff members' names and GDC numbers in an area where it can easily be seen by patients

6.6.11 You should display the following information in an area where it can be easily seen by patients:

- ***the fact that you are regulated by the GDC***
- ***the nine principles contained in this document.*** - **Comment**: Apparently this can be downloaded as a PDF from the GDC to turn into a poster

7.1 You must provide good quality care based on current evidence and authoritative guidance

7.1.1 You must find out about current evidence and best practice which affect your work, premises, equipment and business and follow them. - **Comment**: it's likely impossible to 100% comply with this. It is impossible for you to follow every piece of guidance on every patient every day, and I'll indicate why I think this. Have you read the FGDP guidance on radiography? Can you remember it? Are you supposed to refer to it every time you do a radiograph? How about record keeping? How about the intricacies of NICE guidance? And yet it is a must. I am happy for you to try and prove otherwise.

7.1.2 If you deviate from established practice and guidance, you should record the reasons why and be able to justify your

decision. - **Comment**: The problem here is that much of what we are told to do, as dentists, is contradictory and has little science to back it up. And just to demonstrate this, there are, at my count over 40 ways to fill an occlusal cavity, if you take into account the different liners, bonding systems and materials and techniques available. What I imagine you are being told here is to make sure you are in compliance with Bolam, Bolitho and Montgomery

7.2 You must work within your knowledge, skills, professional competence and abilities

7.2.1 You must only carry out a task or a type of treatment if you are appropriately trained, competent, confident and indemnified. Training can take many different forms. You must be sure that you have undertaken training which is appropriate for you and equips you with the appropriate knowledge and skills to perform a task safely. - **Comment**: Read that again. You will notice the GDC do not define appropriate, so your definition may well be different from theirs. I can guarantee you that a weekend course at Gatwick to learn how to do Implants/short term ortho will unlikely be acceptable to the GDC if something goes wrong. Implant training is now all about mentoring, and anyone who doesn't think ortho will go the same way is living in cloud cuckoo land. Should you be doing short term ortho if you don't know how to do conventional ortho to get you out of a hole if something goes wrong? Talk to your local specialist periodontist and ask them how much buccal recession and implantitis they are being asked to treat (often paid for by the referring clinician) and tell me why the lawyers are having a field day. We are perhaps partly the captains of our own fate here.

7.2.2 You should only deliver treatment and care if you are confident that you have had the necessary training and are

competent to do so. If you are not confident to provide treatment, you must refer the patient to an appropriately trained colleague. - **Comment**: So how do dentists get competent under this standard? You can know the theory but true competence (unconscious competence) doesn't come till you have done 10,000 hours. But if you refer, how do you get the experience to give you the competence. And what about surgical extractions? Where does the GDP go to get experience at this under supervision? Hands on courses are like Hens teeth. And yet, in many areas, the referral pathway only accepts certain criteria. The GDC state that you should only work in your competence, but the NHS expect that you, as a GDP should be able to do everything. CATCH 22 perhaps? I find it somewhat amusing that NHS dentists are castigated for referring treatments they don't like, and yet those working privately are praised for focusing on what they do best. The NHS system is flawed. And there are many who think it is deliberately designed to drive down skills AND drive dentists towards the private sector.

7.2.3 You <u>must</u> only work within your mental and physical capabilities. - **<u>Comment</u>**: You see, this is perhaps the bureaucrats actually trying to help you. Dentists kill themselves by working too many hours, doing the wrong dentistry, treating the wrong patients. If you start to have anxiety, palpitations or back pain (as examples) because of your job, are you breaching the GDC standard if you don't act on this and address it? The GDC perhaps just told you that you have to put your own physical and mental wellbeing first.

7.3 You <u>must</u> update and develop your professional knowledge and skills throughout your working life

7.3.2 You <u>should</u> take part in activities that maintain update or develop your knowledge and skills. Your continuing professional development (CPD) activity should improve your practice. For more information, see the GDC's advice on CPD. - **<u>Comment</u>**: Your CPD should improve your practice.

And this means that going on courses on topics you like is less important than going on courses on stuff you need improvement in. And the more knowledge you gain, the more you can defend yourself against a claim of impropriety. You will meet more people, gain more knowledge, and start to form a mastermind alliance around you. You might even start to really love the job. Crazier things have happened.

8.2 You must act promptly if patients or colleagues are at risk and take measures to protect them

8.2.3 Where possible, you should raise concerns first with your employer or manager. However, it may not always be appropriate or possible to raise concerns with them, particularly if they are the source of your concern. - **Comment**: Here we have evidence of an approach to local resolution. There should be more importance on this when it comes to the FtP process.

8.2.6 You must refer concerns about other healthcare professionals to the relevant regulator. - **Comment**: This is an interesting one. I have concerns about the ability of every GDP in the country to deal with the broken system they find themselves in. And if a lab routinely gets impressions that are completely shocking, what do you think they now have to do under this Standard?

9.1 You must ensure that your conduct, both at work and in your personal life, justifies patients' trust in you and the public's trust in the dental profession

9.1.1 You must treat all team members, other colleagues and members of the public fairly, with dignity and in line with the law. - **Comment**: You must treat all team members, other colleagues and members of the public fairly, with dignity and in line with the law. Well doesn't that run both ways. Are the GDC treating us with dignity?

9.1.3 You should not publish anything that could affect patients' and the public's confidence in you, or the dental profession, in any public media, unless this is done as part of raising a concern. Public media includes social networking sites, blogs and other social media. In particular, you must not make personal, inaccurate or derogatory comments about patients or colleagues. See our guidance on social networking for more information. - **Comment**: The GDC have a whole separate guidance on the use of Social media.

Much of the standards issued by the GDC are self-explanatory. Remember to access the supplemental standards and guidance they issue:

Scope of Practice[9]

Direct access[10]

Indemnity[11]

Medical emergencies[12]

Also check out **Appendix 12** for instances when the GDC arguably get it wrong.

Legionella

Before the CQC came along, many dental practices didn't see this as an issue. But there is actual official guidance governing the testing and prevention of legionella[14]. To comply with CQC and HSE requirements, you will need to follow:

- **The HSE approved code of practice and Guidance L8**[15]

- **The Health Technical Memorandum (HTM) 04-01: Safe Water in healthcare premises[16]**
- **The HTM 01-05: Decontamination in primary care dental practices, specifically Chapter 19**

If you are planning on selling your practice, this will be one of the many things the buyers will look for in their due diligence. They WILL ask for it, so get it done as soon as possible if you have to date "forgotten".

Medical Emergency drugs and equipment

Dental practices and their teams are expected to follow the guidance set out by the UK resuscitation council[17] (GDC Standard 1.5.3 - You must follow the guidance on medical emergencies and training updates issued by the Resuscitation Council UK). This is the summary for advice from the Resuscitation Council:

- **"Cardiorespiratory arrest is rare in primary dental practice.**
- **There is a public expectation that dental practitioners and all other dental care professionals should be competent in treating cardiorespiratory arrest.**
- **All primary care dental facilities should have a process for medical risk-assessment of their patients.**
- **Specific resuscitation equipment should be available immediately in all primary care dental premises. This equipment list should be standardised throughout the UK.**
- **All clinical areas should have immediate access to an automated external defibrillator (AED).**
- **Primary dental care providers, general dental practitioners and all other dental healthcare**

professionals should undergo training in cardiopulmonary resuscitation (CPR) including basic airway management and the use of an AED.

- **Each primary dental care facility should have a plan for summoning assistance in the event of a cardiorespiratory arrest. For most practices this will mean calling 999 immediately.**
- **There should be regular practice and teaching using simulation-based cardiorespiratory arrest scenarios.**
- **Dental staffs' knowledge and skills in resuscitation should be updated at least annually."**

Please consult the resuscitation website for the rest of their guidance. Whilst I could post the recommended drug kit contents, I am mindful that it changes regularly and thus may be out of date by the time you read this book. The same information can also be obtained from the CQC page Dental Mysthbusters 4[18].

Radiography

The provision of Radiographs comes under CQC regulations 15 and 17. They are also governed by the **Ionising Radiations Regulations 1999 (IRR99)**[19] and the **Ionising Radiation (Medical Exposure) Regulations 2000 (IR(ME)R 2000)**[20]. There are several key points to take from these regulations:

- HSE must be notified 28 days before:
  - when dental X-ray equipment is installed
  - where there is a change of premises or a change of ownership of the practice
  - when there has been a 'material change' in the use of ionising radiation

- Radiation Protection Adviser (RPA) - Individuals and organisations recognised as RPA bodies are listed on the HSE website. There is some debate as to whether you need one under contract or whether you can pay for advice on a case by case basis. The HSE in your area can advise on this
- Radiation Protection Supervisor - usually a dentist at the practice but it can be a suitably qualified dental nurse/hygienist/therapist
- Local Rules specific to each machine must be displayed
- There must be a prior risk assessment, restriction of exposure, maintenance and examining of engineering controls, contingency plans, controlled areas all recorded and logged
- Critical Examination Packs and Acceptance Tests must be undertaken
- Proper training must be provided to all persons associated with dental radiography.
- There should be a Q&A program in place for radiographs
- Machines should be inspected by a suitably qualified individual every three years
- IRMER 2000 states that GDC registrants should do 5 hours of suitable CPD in radiography in every 5-year cycle
- The provision of radiographs must be regularly audited

Recruitment

Yep you guessed it, there are rules over the recruitment of health care staff. These are outlined in the **Health and Social Care Act 2008 (Regulated Activities) Regulations 2014 (Schedule 3)**[21]. I will decipher it for you (this is what the CQC will expect to see when they come around):

From **CQC Myth busters 19:**[22]

For all staff:

- **Proof of identity including a recent photograph (for a small organisation that really makes no sense whatsoever, but it's there in the legislation)**
- **A full employment history with explanations for gaps in employment (unless joined the practice pre 2008)**
- **Documentary evidence of qualifications relevant to the duties that person is expected to perform**
- **Information about any physical or mental health conditions relevant to a person's capability, after reasonable adjustments are made, to properly carry out tasks they are expected to perform (for GDC registrants only)**

Receptionists and administrators:

- **Copy or evidence of standard DBS check**

Dentists, dental nurses and hygienists:

- **Copy or evidence of an enhanced DBS check**

Staff working with vulnerable children or adults:

- **Satisfactory evidence of conduct in previous employment relating to health or social care, or children or vulnerable adults**
- **If staff have been previously employed in a position involving work with children or vulnerable adults, satisfactory verification why their employment in that position ended**

With regards DBS checks, it is debatable as to whether there is actually any "LAW" that says these are mandatory. I have communication from the CQC that says that there are not, BUT, you are expected to be able to justify why you have not done so for all staff who are exposed to children and vulnerable adults. At the very least you need an in depth risk assessment and crossed fingers in the hope the CQC inspectors don't pull you up on it. The advice is therefore to get the DBS checks done. Risk assessments must also be done if you are awaiting the results of DBS checks.

Safeguarding

There are a lot of systemic failures occurring across the country regarding this. The grooming scandals in multiple cities (that should really have caused a bigger uproar in the media) are a reflection of the problem. The state, as a whole has been slow to adapt, and recent improvements in safeguarding are encouraging. As the GDC standards state:

8.5 You must take appropriate action if you have concerns about the possible abuse of children or vulnerable adults
8.5.1 You must raise any concerns you may have about the possible abuse or neglect of children or vulnerable adults. You must know who to contact for further advice and how to refer concerns to an appropriate authority such as your local social services department.
8.5.2 You must find out about local procedures for the protection of children and vulnerable adults. You must follow these procedures if you suspect that a child or vulnerable adult might be at risk because of abuse or neglect. See our website for further information.

The GDC have introduced specific guidance on reporting Female Genital Mutilation[23] as there is a perceived chance dentists may uncover such practices through the conversations they have and overhear. You should also familiarise yourself with official government guidance called "**Mandatory reporting of female genital mutilation: procedural information**"[24]

With regards to the CQC, this relates to **Regulation 13: Safeguarding service users from abuse and improper treatment**:

13.—
1. Service users must be protected from abuse and improper treatment in accordance with this regulation.
2. Systems and processes must be established and operated effectively to prevent abuse of service users.
3. Systems and processes must be established and operated effectively to investigate, immediately upon becoming aware of, any allegation or evidence of such abuse.
4. Care or treatment for service users must not be provided in a way that—

> ***a. includes discrimination against a service user on grounds of any protected characteristic (as defined in section 4 of the Equality Act 2010) of the service user,***
> ***b. includes acts intended to control or restrain a service user that are not necessary to prevent, or not a proportionate response to, a risk of harm posed to the service user or another individual if the service user was not subject to control or restraint,***
> ***c. is degrading for the service user, or***
> ***d. significantly disregards the needs of the service user for care or treatment.***

5. A service user must not be deprived of their liberty for the purpose of receiving care or treatment without lawful authority.
6. For the purposes of this regulation 'abuse' means—

a. any behaviour towards a service user that is an offence under the Sexual Offences Act 2003(a),
b. ill-treatment (whether of a physical or psychological nature) of a service user,
c. theft, misuse or misappropriation of money or property belonging to a service user, or
d. neglect of a service user.

7. For the purposes of this regulation, a person controls or restrains a service user if that person—
a. uses, or threatens to use, force to secure the doing of an act which the service user resists, or
b. restricts the service user's liberty of movement, whether or not the service user resists, including by use of physical, mechanical or chemical means.

This regulation requires you and your staff to be able to demonstrate an understanding of which individuals are potentially at risk as well as a knowledge of the types of abuse you may see. There needs to be internal arrangements for raising and recording safeguarding concerns as well as a means of reporting externally.

Probably the best document to help you with this is the 2009 DOH book "**Child protection and the Dental Team.**"[25] The flowchart can be found in **Appendix 9.**

Additionally, the CQC will expect dental practices to follow the 2014 guidance laid out "**Safeguarding children and young people: roles and competences for health care staff - intercollegiate document**"[26]. This sets out the minimum training requirements required for safeguarding that should take place every three years

Level 1: Non-clinical staff

Level 2: Dentists and DCP's

Level 3: Paediatric dentists/orthodontists

Sedation

If you do conscious sedation, and many practices no longer do, there are certain requirements to follow:

Standards for Conscious Sedation in the Provision of Dental Care, RCS (2015)[27]

Society for the Advancement of Anaesthesia (SAAD) checklist (2015)[28]

The Rest References

1. **Equality Act 2010** - http://www.legislation.gov.uk/ukpga/2010/15/contents
2. **RCS: Methodologies for Clinical Audit in Dentistry** - https://www.rcseng.ac.uk/library-and-publications/college-publications/docs/methodologies-for-clinical-audit-in-dentistry/
3. **HTM 01-05** - https://www.gov.uk/government/uploads/system/uploads/attachment_data/file/170689/HTM_01-05_2013.pdf
4. **Health and Social Care Act 2008: Code of Practice on the prevention and control of infections and related guidance** - https://www.gov.uk/government/publications/the-health-and-social-care-act-2008-code-of-practice-on-the-prevention-and-control-of-infections-and-related-guidance
5. **Pressure Systems Safety Regulations 2000** - http://www.legislation.gov.uk/uksi/2000/128/contents/made
6. **Cross infection audit tool** - https://www.gov.uk/government/publications/decontamination-in-primary-care-dental-practices
7. **Equality Act 2010** - https://www.legislation.gov.uk/ukpga/2010/15/contents
8. **DOH: Delivering Oral health** - https://www.gov.uk/government/publications/delivering-better-oral-health-an-evidence-based-toolkit-for-prevention

9. **GDC: Scope of Practice** - https://www.gdc-uk.org/professionals/standards/st-scope-of-practice
10. **GDC: Direct access** - https://www.gdc-uk.org/professionals/standards/direct-access
11. **GDC: Indemnity** - https://www.gdc-uk.org/professionals/standards/indemnity
12. **GDC: Medical emergencies** - https://www.gdc-uk.org/professionals/standards/medical-emergencies
13. **Preparing for the GDPR** - https://ico.org.uk/media/1624219/preparing-for-the-gdpr-12-steps.pdf
14. http://www.hse.gov.uk/legionnaires/
15. **The HSE approved code of practice and Guidance L8** - http://www.hse.gov.uk/pubns/books/l8.htm
16. **The Health Technical Memorandum (HTM) 04-01: Safe Water in healthcare premises** - https://www.gov.uk/government/uploads/system/uploads/attachment_data/file/524880/DH_HTM_0401_PART_A_acc.pdf
17. **Primary Dental Care Quality Standards for CPR** - https://www.resus.org.uk/quality-standards/primary-dental-care-quality-standards-for-cpr/
18. **CQC: Mythbusters 4** - http://www.cqc.org.uk/guidance-providers/dentists/dental-mythbuster-4-drugs-equipment-required-medical-emergency
19. **Ionising Radiations Regulations 1999 (IRR99)** - http://www.legislation.gov.uk/uksi/1999/3232/contents/made
20. **Ionising Radiation (Medical Exposure) Regulations 2000 (IR(ME)R 2000)** - https://www.gov.uk/government/publications/the-ionising-radiation-medical-exposure-regulations-2000
21. **Health and Social Care Act 2008 (Regulated Activities) Regulations 2014 (Schedule 3)** -

http://www.legislation.gov.uk/uksi/2014/2936/schedule/3/made

22. **CQC Myth busters 19** - http://www.cqc.org.uk/guidance-providers/dentists/dental-mythbuster-19-staff-recruitment-information
23. **GDC: Reporting Female Genital Mutilation** - https://gdc-uk.org/newsarticle?id=932
24. **Mandatory reporting of female genital mutilation: procedural information** - https://www.gov.uk/government/publications/mandatory-reporting-of-female-genital-mutilation-procedural-information
25. **Child protection and the Dental Team** - https://bda.org/childprotection/Resources/Documents/Childprotectionandthedentalteam_v1_4_Nov09.pdf
26. **Safeguarding children and young people: roles and competences for health care staff - intercollegiate document** - http://www.ehcap.co.uk/content/sites/ehcap/uploads/NewsDocuments/199/Safeguarding-Children-Roles-and-Competences-for-Healthcare-Staff--02-0----2.PDF
27. **Standards for Conscious Sedation in the Provision of Dental Care, RCS (2015)** - http://www.saad.org.uk/images/Linked-IACSD-2015.pdf
28. **Society for the Advancement of Anaesthesia (SAAD) checklist (2015)** - http://www.saad.org.uk/images/Linked-Safe-Practice-Scheme-Website-L.pdf

Scenarios

Scenario 1

Mr Miggins phones your practice and asks your reception team what time his wife's appointment is. Can you tell him? Do your reception team know how to deal with this?

Scenario 2

You need to phone a different Mr Miggins (there are a lot of them at your practice) to re-arrange his appointment that afternoon because the dentist is ill and they have only provided one phone number. He doesn't answer but his wife does because he is "indisposed". Do you leave her a message to be passed on?

Things to consider:

- How do you know that it's his wife?
- Has Mr Miggins given you specific consent to discuss information with his wife?
- Are you allowed to even tell Mrs Miggins who you are?

Scenario 3

A fifteen-year-old arrives for an examination with someone you have never seen before (he usually comes with his Mother). The child is Gillick competent and able to consent to examination, and it turns out that the adult with them is a "neighbour". You need to convey information to the child's parent AND book an appointment for treatment. You have also spotted a suspicious lesion in the child's mouth. How do you convey the information that needs conveying to the mother whilst maintaining confidentiality?

Things to consider:

- What information, if anything, can you give to the neighbour?
- Can the neighbour book the child's next appointment?
- Is there anything you can do to stop this scenario happening in the future?

Scenario 4

Mrs Miggins has her teeth veneered and develops extreme sensitivity that requires root canal treatment. Under Bolam the court would look at your treatment to make sure it met the required standard and would ask a reasonable body of opinion if this outcome was something you should have warned against. Montgomery looks at whether the patient would have wanted to know that risk beforehand. So even if half the dentists in the country are of the opinion that the risk is so low as to not be worth mentioning, if the patient needed to know that risk then the case of negligence against you would likely go forward because you had breached the standard of care in the realms of consent.

- Do you know how to obtain consent under Montgomery?

Scenario 5

You are doing a root filling on Mr Jones. You push a little bit too hard on the Hypochlorite syringe and the patient reports intense pain and starts to develop swelling under the eye.

- Do you have a system to deal with this?

- What actions do you need to take?
- Who do you need to notify that this event has occurred?

Scenario 6

A patient has been aggressive to you and your staff. It is bad enough that you feel you need to notify the police.

- What systems do you have in place to deal with this scenario?
- Who do you need to contact as well as the police?
- What possible medical conditions could cause this scenario?

Scenario 7

Your 3.45 molar endo patient has cancelled and you have an hour free. You decide to go through the old record cards and discard those that are out of date.

- What system do you have in place for doing this?
- How do you propose to dispose of the records?
- How do you dispose of electronic records that are beyond the time limit?
-

Scenario 8

A disgruntled Miss Miggins makes a freedom of Information act, asking for details of the monetary value of your NHS contract.

- Do you have a FOIA policy?
- What information do you need to provide?
- Are you going to charge? If so how much?

Scenario 9

You see a new patient and are dismayed by the amount of caries present in the patients mouth. There are also numerous periodontal pockets. When you inform the patient, they seem surprised and upset. In your dental history, you note that the patient had been a regular attender at a practice down the road, and you have seen a few patients like this attend from that practice. The patient asks "how come my mouth is so bad, did my last dentist miss it all?"

- What information do you give the patient?
- Who, if anyone, should you contact?
- Do you feel being critical of the last dentist is the way to go?

Scenario 10

A patient complains that their confidentiality was breached by your receptionist.

- How do ensure confidentiality for your patients in each part of your practice?
- How do you respond to the complaint

Please note the "Miggins" used in all these examples is fictional.

Appendix 1: Example GDC charges

These are the sort of things that appear on charge sheets indicating that a registrant's fitness to practise is impaired

- You failed to carry out sufficient diagnostic assessments
- You failed to carry out sufficient pre-treatment investigations
- You failed to carry out sufficient treatment planning
- You failed to adequately communicate the treatment plan to the patient
- You provided a poor standard of treatment at X (for example, crowns, fillings etc.)
- You failed to diagnose Y
- You failed to treat/undertreat
- You failed to provide adequate preventative treatment
- You failed with regards your radiographic practice
- You failed to give adequate advice in relation to oral health
- You carried out treatment that was not clinically indicated
- You failed in your antibiotic prescribing practice
- You did not discuss the full risks and benefits of the proposed treatment
- You did not ensure the patient understood the risk of treatment
- You did not provide the patient with all the treatment options
- You did not provide the patient the opportunity to discuss treatment options
- You did not advise the patient of the cost of treatment
- You failed to refer, accept an inappropriate referral etc.
- You did not provide sufficient post-operative instructions
- You left the patient without continuity of care

- Failures in the provision of conscious sedation
- You did not ensure that a contingency plan was in place to cover dental emergencies whilst you were away from the practice
- You did not use rubber dam when indicated
- You restored a tooth with glass ionomer when it was not clinically indicated
- You failed to maintain an adequate standard of record keeping
- You failed to write a written report for your radiographs
- You failed to provide patient X with adequate access to their dental records
- You are insufficiently fluent in written and/or spoken English to communicate effectively as a (dentist/dental care professional) in the United Kingdom
- You failed to adequately respond to a patient's complaint about their dental treatment
- You failed to treat the patient with dignity and respect
- You failed to treat the patient with kindness and compassion
- You failed to communicate with the patient in a professional manner
- You failed to respond adequately to a patient's concern about their treatment
- You discriminated against a patient with regards X
- You failed to obtain informed consent for the treatment provided
- You failed to protect the patient's confidentiality
- You lost patient records belonging to the patient
- You failed to display a price list in the reception or waiting area of the practice
- The cost of treatment was different to what the price list states
- You failed to display a price list on your practice website

- You provided information to the patient that was misleading and dishonest
- You provided treatment to NHS patients when you were not included on a performer's list
- You told your employer that you had notified the GDC of your convictions when you had not
- Your behaviour was inappropriate towards X in that your behaviour was unprofessional/sexually motivated
- Your actions put a patient's safety at risk
- That being a registered dentist you accepted a caution at X police station
- You have not complied with the terms of a court order
- That you failed to declare your convictions to the GDC
- That you failed to declare to the GDC that you were charged with X
- That you misappropriated monies from practice X
- That you forged a certificate for a course you never attended
- You made a false claim to the NHS that you suffered from X health condition
- You worked outside your scope of practice
- You failed to ensure that your dental nurse was adequately trained
- You failed to maintain adequate standards of cross infection control
- Etc
- Etc
- Etc

Appendix 2: GDC Mandated CPD Requirements

Enhanced CPD - https://www.gdc-uk.org/professionals/cpd/enhanced-cpd

The GDC will inform you when the changes to CPD requirements need to be implemented. The new requirements are outlined below:

- Develop a personal development plan which will lay out the CPD done and allow the registrant to reflect on their learnings
- Record the CPD done with evidence.
- Dentists must do 100 hours of Verifiable CPD in a 10-year cycle
- Do at least 10 hours over any 2-year cycle

What are the changes to the verifiable criteria?

In order for CPD to be considered verifiable, the evidence (e.g. certificates) given by CPD providers must include the following:

- The subject, learning content, aims, and objectives;
- The anticipated GDC development outcomes of the CPD;
- The date that the CPD was undertaken;
- The total number of hours CPD undertaken;
- The name of the practitioner who has participated in the CPD activity;
- That the CPD is subject to quality assurance, with the name of the person or body providing the quality assurance;

- Confirmation from the provider that the information contained in it is full and accurate.
- It should also include the participant's registration number.

A CPD statement is a confirmation that you must submit every year to confirm that your declaration is accurate and that you have met the requirements set out in the CPD rules. When you make your statement, you will be prompted to confirm that:

- the number of hours you have undertaken in that year, or if you have done no hours in that year, then confirm you have done zero hours;
- you have kept a CPD record;
- the CPD undertaken is relevant to your field of practice;
- that the information you have provided is full and accurate.
- Your statement will not be compliant unless you confirm all the above.

A CPD record is the documentary evidence demonstrating each item of CPD you have undertaken. This comprises of a personal development plan and log of all CPD activity you complete. You only need to show us your CPD record if we specifically ask you for it. Your CPD record should contain:

- a personal development plan which details all the CPD you plan to undertake, the development outcomes that you aim to meet and timeframe for completing the CPD. This should be created at the start of your cycle and adapted throughout your cycle as your needs change,

- a log of the CPD you undertook- including the date it was undertaken, number of hours gained from each CPD activity
- the evidence (e.g. certificate) you gained from the providers for each CPD activity
- the development outcomes mapped against all planned and completed CPD activity.

Based on Statutory Instrument **2017 No. 966**

HEALTH CARE AND ASSOCIATED PROFESSIONS

The General Dental Council (Continuing Professional Development) (Dentists and Dental Care Professionals) Rules

Order of Council 2017

Appendix 3: Consent for image capture and storage (written by Victoria Holden and reproduced with permission)

Patient Name:______________________**Date of Birth:**_________

I consent that photographic images (including of x-rays, models and videos) of me (or under 16 child of which I am parent or legal guardian) may be taken and used in perpetuity for the following purpose(s) for which I understand that it may not be possible for me to subsequently withdraw consent. I understand that I do not hold any copyright or any other rights in the photographs taken and do not expect compensation, financial or otherwise, for their use. I understand that my name and any other identifying information will be kept confidential.

Images may be used for the purposes listed below. We must have Level 1 consent to be able to store your images. Please delete anything at Level 2 or 3 consent you are not comfortable to provide:

Level 1 (*Confidential record only*)

Storage as part of confidential patient dental records.

Level 2 (*Restricted educational use*)

(a) Clinical teaching and/or research, and shown only to appropriate clinical staff and students and/or displayed for use by staff and students following a course of study on a restricted access educational or institutional website.

(b) Demonstration to patients of treatment modalities.

Level 3 (*Open publication*)

(a) Publication in a professional journal or textbook, and/or as part of a lecture.

(b) Publication in marketing or promotional literature.

(c) Publication on open access websites (open access means making available and communicating to anyone worldwide, including but not limited to clinical professionals and includes social media sites such as Facebook, Twitter, Instagram and Snapchat). The publication on open access websites may, but not necessarily, form part of a course where users will download content onto any device for their personal and non-commercial use.

I confirm that I am over 16.

I confirm that I am the parent /legal guardian of

____

Signed ______________________________________

Date: ____________________

Appendix 4: IOC information

Information to be published	How the information can be obtained	Cost
Class 1 - Who we are and what we do (Organisational information, structures, locations and contacts) -This will be current information only		
Who's who in the practice		
Contact details for the practice (named contacts where possible with telephone number and email address (if used))		
Opening hours		
Class 2 – What we spend and how we spend it (Financial information relating to projected and actual income and expenditure, procurement, contracts and financial audit) Current and previous financial		

year as a minimum		
Details on NHS funding received by the practice and the cost of operating the NHS contract. We would expect dentists to consider publishing as much information as possible, including as much detail as possible.		
Total annual expenditure on the provision of our contracted services (since most practices also provide care to patients on a private basis, the costs have been apportioned)		
Audit of NHS income, if held		
Class 3 – What our priorities are and how we are doing (Strategies and plans, performance indicators, audits, inspections and reviews) - Current and previous year as a minimum		

Plans for the development and provision of NHS services		
Performance data including performance against targets		
Practice inspection. Inspection reports by regulators (for England: the Care Quality Commission (CQC); Wales: Healthcare Inspectorate Wales; or Northern Ireland: the Regulation and Quality Improvement Authority (RQIA))		
Class 4 – How we make decisions (Decision making processes and records of decisions) - Current and previous year as a minimum		
Records of decisions made in the practice/firm affecting the provision of NHS services.		
Class 5 – Our policies and		

procedures (Current written protocols, policies and procedures for delivering our services and responsibilities) - Current information only. Here we have listed the policies we would expect practices to have. Any additional policies should also be listed. Mark "not held" against any policies that are not actually held.		
Policies and procedures about customer service		
Policies and procedures about employment of staff		
Equality and diversity policy		
Health and safety policy		
Infection control policy		
Radiation protection checklist		
Complaints procedures (including those covering requests for information and operating the		

publication scheme)		
Records management policies (records retention, destruction and archive)		
Confidentiality and data protection policies		
Policies and procedures for handling requests for information		
Practice information leaflet		
Class 6 – Lists and Registers Currently maintained lists and registers only		
We recognise that it is unlikely that dentists are going to have registers available for public inspection and while this remains the case "none held" can be entered in this section.		
Any publicly available register or list (if any are held this should be publicised; in most circumstances existing access provisions will suffice).		

Class 7 – The services we offer (Information about the services we offer, including leaflets, guidance and newsletters produced for the public) - Current information only		
The services provided under contract to the NHS		
Charges for any of these services		
Information leaflets		
Out of hours arrangements		

Appendix 5: Sharing of information form

Patient Name:

Date:

Yep you guessed it, yet another form for you to fill out. Due to all the rules and regulations we now have to abide by, it is important that we do everything by the book. Because of data protection laws, consent laws and privacy issues, we need to know how you'd like to be contacted regarding your treatment and finances. Unfortunately this is now the world we live in. Sorry.

Treatment issues might include x-ray results, treatment plans, specialist referrals, etc. We also need to know if it is acceptable to leave you voice mails or talk to your spouse regarding your treatment/appointments.

If you are over 18 but your parents are still responsible for your bill here, please check off permissions allowing us to discuss your treatment and finances with them. If there is anyone else with whom we may discuss your care, for example your adult child, please put their name in the space marked "Other". If the phone numbers or email address below are missing or incorrect, please put the correct ones in the space at the bottom of the form.

It is acceptable to contact me regarding dental treatment issues via (Please circle your MOST preferred method of contact):

Please tick on the right ALL methods that are acceptable.

Email

____

Home telephone Ok to leave voice mail Y/N

____

Work telephone Ok to leave voice mail Y/N

____

Mobile phone Ok to leave voice mail Y/N

____

It is acceptable to talk to the following people about TREATMENT/APPOINTMENT issues:

My spouse Name:

My parents Name:

Other: Name:

It is acceptable to talk to the following people about FINANCIAL issues:

My spouse Name:

My parents Name:

Other: Name:

Please put any corrections to phone numbers or email address here:

If you wish to change any of your consent to these aspects please contact us at [ ]

Appendix 6: CPR

Civil Procedure Rules - Rules and Directions -Part 35 Experts and Assessors

Duty to restrict expert evidence

35.1 Expert evidence shall be restricted to that which is reasonably required to resolve the proceedings.

Interpretation and definitions

35.2 (1) A reference to an 'expert' in this Part is a reference to a person who has been instructed to give or prepare expert evidence for the purpose of proceedings.

(2) 'Single joint expert' means an expert instructed to prepare a report for the court on behalf of two or more of the parties (including the claimant) to the proceedings.

Experts – overriding duty to the court

35.3 (1) It is the duty of experts to help the court on matters within their expertise.

(2) This duty overrides any obligation to the person from whom experts have received instructions or by whom they are paid.

Court's power to restrict expert evidence

35.4 (1) No party may call an expert or put in evidence an expert's report without the court's permission.

(2) When parties apply for permission they must provide an estimate of the costs of the proposed expert evidence and identify –

(a) the field in which expert evidence is required and the issues which the expert evidence will address; and

(b) where practicable, the name of the proposed expert.

(3) If permission is granted it shall be in relation only to the expert named or the field identified under paragraph (2). The order granting permission may specify the issues which the expert evidence should address.

(3A) Where a claim has been allocated to the small claims track or the fast track, if permission is given for expert evidence, it will normally be given for evidence from only one expert on a particular issue.

(3B) In a soft tissue injury claim, permission—

(a) may normally only be given for one expert medical report;

(b) may not be given initially unless the medical report is a fixed cost medical report. Where the claimant seeks permission to obtain a further medical report, if the report is from a medical expert in any of the following disciplines—

(i) Consultant Orthopaedic Surgeon;

(ii) Consultant in Accident and Emergency Medicine;

(iii) General Practitioner registered with the General Medical Council; or

(iv) Physiotherapist registered with the Health and Care Professions Council, the report must be a fixed cost medical report.

(3C) In this rule, 'fixed cost medical report' and 'soft tissue injury claim' have the same meaning as in paragraph 1.1(10A) and (16A), respectively, of the RTA Protocol.

(Paragraph 7 of Practice Direction 35 sets out some of the circumstances the court will consider when deciding whether expert evidence should be given by a single joint expert.)

(4) The court may limit the amount of a party's expert's fees and expenses that may be recovered from any other party.

General requirement for expert evidence to be given in a written report

35.5 (1) Expert evidence is to be given in a written report unless the court directs otherwise.

(2) If a claim is on the small claims track or the fast track, the court will not direct an expert to attend a hearing unless it is necessary to do so in the interests of justice.

Written questions to experts

35.6 (1) A party may put written questions about an expert's report (which must be proportionate) to –

(a) an expert instructed by another party; or

(b) a single joint expert appointed under rule 35.7.

(2) Written questions under paragraph (1) –

(a) may be put once only;

(b) must be put within 28 days of service of the expert's report; and

(c) must be for the purpose only of clarification of the report,

unless in any case –

(i) the court gives permission; or

(ii) the other party agrees.

(3) An expert's answers to questions put in accordance with paragraph (1) shall be treated as part of the expert's report.

(4) Where –

(a) a party has put a written question to an expert instructed by another party; and

(b) the expert does not answer that question,

the court may make one or both of the following orders in relation to the party who instructed the expert –

(i) that the party may not rely on the evidence of that expert; or

(ii) that the party may not recover the fees and expenses of that expert from any other party.

Court's power to direct that evidence is to be given by a single joint expert

35.7 (1) Where two or more parties wish to submit expert evidence on a particular issue, the court may direct that the evidence on that issue is to be given by a single joint expert.

(2) Where the parties who wish to submit the evidence ('the relevant parties') cannot agree who should be the single joint expert, the court may –

(a) select the expert from a list prepared or identified by the relevant parties; or

(b) direct that the expert be selected in such other manner as the court may direct.

Instructions to a single joint expert

35.8 (1) Where the court gives a direction under rule 35.7 for a single joint expert to be used, any relevant party may give instructions to the expert.

(2) When a party gives instructions to the expert that party must, at the same time, send a copy to the other relevant parties.

(3) The court may give directions about –

(a) the payment of the expert's fees and expenses; and

(b) any inspection, examination or experiments which the expert wishes to carry out.

(4) The court may, before an expert is instructed –

(a) limit the amount that can be paid by way of fees and expenses to the expert; and

(b) direct that some or all of the relevant parties pay that amount into court.

(5) Unless the court otherwise directs, the relevant parties are jointly and severally liable(GL) for the payment of the expert's fees and expenses.

Power of court to direct a party to provide information

35.9 Where a party has access to information which is not reasonably available to another party, the court may direct the party who has access to the information to –

(a) prepare and file a document recording the information; and

(b) serve a copy of that document on the other party.

Contents of report

35.10 (1) An expert's report must comply with the requirements set out in Practice Direction 35.

(2) At the end of an expert's report there must be a statement that the expert understands and has complied with their duty to the court.

(3) The expert's report must state the substance of all material instructions, whether written or oral, on the basis of which the report was written.

(4) The instructions referred to in paragraph (3) shall not be privileged(GL) against disclosure but the court will not, in relation to those instructions –

(a) order disclosure of any specific document; or

(b) permit any questioning in court, other than by the party who instructed the expert,

unless it is satisfied that there are reasonable grounds to consider the statement of instructions given under paragraph (3) to be inaccurate or incomplete.

Use by one party of expert's report disclosed by another

35.11 Where a party has disclosed an expert's report, any party may use that expert's report as evidence at the trial.

Discussions between experts

35.12 (1) The court may, at any stage, direct a discussion between experts for the purpose of requiring the experts to –

(a) identify and discuss the expert issues in the proceedings; and

(b) where possible, reach an agreed opinion on those issues.

(2) The court may specify the issues which the experts must discuss.

(3) The court may direct that following a discussion between the experts they must prepare a statement for the court setting out those issues on which –

(a) they agree; and

(b) they disagree, with a summary of their reasons for disagreeing.

(4) The content of the discussion between the experts shall not be referred to at the trial unless the parties agree.

(5) Where experts reach agreement on an issue during their discussions, the agreement shall not bind the parties unless the parties expressly agree to be bound by the agreement.

Consequence of failure to disclose expert's report

35.13 A party who fails to disclose an expert's report may not use the report at the trial or call the expert to give evidence orally unless the court gives permission.

Expert's right to ask court for directions

35.14 (1) Experts may file written requests for directions for the purpose of assisting them in carrying out their functions.

(2) Experts must, unless the court orders otherwise, provide copies of the proposed requests for directions under paragraph (1) –

(a) to the party instructing them, at least 7 days before they file the requests; and

(b) to all other parties, at least 4 days before they file them.

(3) The court, when it gives directions, may also direct that a party be served with a copy of the directions.

Assessors

35.15 (1) This rule applies where the court appoints one or more persons under section 70 of the Senior Courts Act 19811 or section 63 of the County Courts Act 19842as an assessor.

(2) An assessor will assist the court in dealing with a matter in which the assessor has skill and experience.

(3) An assessor will take such part in the proceedings as the court may direct and in particular the court may direct an assessor to –

(a) prepare a report for the court on any matter at issue in the proceedings; and

(b) attend the whole or any part of the trial to advise the court on any such matter.

(4) If an assessor prepares a report for the court before the trial has begun –

(a) the court will send a copy to each of the parties; and

(b) the parties may use it at trial.

(5) The remuneration to be paid to an assessor is to be determined by the court and will form part of the costs of the proceedings.

(6) The court may order any party to deposit in the court office a specified sum in respect of an assessor's fees and, where it does so, the assessor will not be asked to act until the sum has been deposited.

(7) Paragraphs (5) and (6) do not apply where the remuneration of the assessor is to be paid out of money provided by Parliament.

In addition to this, there is supplemental instructions for expert witnesses:

Introduction

1 Part 35 is intended to limit the use of oral expert evidence to that which is reasonably required. In addition, where possible, matters requiring expert evidence should be dealt with by only one expert. Experts and those instructing them are expected to have regard to the guidance contained in the Guidance for the Instruction of Experts in Civil Claims 2014 at www.judiciary.gov.uk. (Further guidance on experts is contained in Annex C to the Practice Direction (Pre-Action Conduct)).

Expert Evidence – General Requirements

2.1 Expert evidence should be the independent product of the expert uninfluenced by the pressures of litigation.

2.2 Experts should assist the court by providing objective, unbiased opinions on matters within their expertise, and should not assume the role of an advocate.

2.3 Experts should consider all material facts, including those which might detract from their opinions.

2.4 Experts should make it clear –

(a) when a question or issue falls outside their expertise; and

(b) when they are not able to reach a definite opinion, for example because they have insufficient information.

2.5 If, after producing a report, an expert's view changes on any material matter, such change of view should be communicated to all the parties without delay, and when appropriate to the court.

2.6 (1) In a soft tissue injury claim, where permission is given for a fixed cost medical report, the first report must be obtained from an accredited medical expert selected via the MedCo Portal (website at: www.medco.org.uk).

(2) The cost of obtaining a further report from an expert not listed in rule 35.4(3C)(a) to (d) is not subject to rules 45.19(2A)(b) or 45.29I(2A)(b), but the use of that expert and the cost must be justified.

(3) 'Accredited medical expert', 'fixed cost medical report', 'MedCo', and 'soft tissue injury claim' have the same meaning as in paragraph 1.1(A1), (10A), (12A) and (16A), respectively, of the RTA Protocol.

Form and Content of an Expert's Report

3.1 An expert's report should be addressed to the court and not to the party from whom the expert has received instructions.

3.2 An expert's report must:

(1) give details of the expert's qualifications;

(2) give details of any literature or other material which has been relied on in making the report;

(3) contain a statement setting out the substance of all facts and instructions which are material to the opinions expressed in the report or upon which those opinions are based;

(4) make clear which of the facts stated in the report are within the expert's own knowledge;

(5) say who carried out any examination, measurement, test or experiment which the expert has used for the report, give the qualifications of that person, and say whether or not the test or experiment has been carried out under the expert's supervision;

(6) where there is a range of opinion on the matters dealt with in the report –

(a) summarise the range of opinions; and

(b) give reasons for the expert's own opinion;

(7) contain a summary of the conclusions reached;

(8) if the expert is not able to give an opinion without qualification, state the qualification; and

(9) contain a statement that the expert –

(a) understands their duty to the court, and has complied with that duty; and

(b) is aware of the requirements of Part 35, this practice direction and the Guidance for the Instruction of Experts in Civil Claims 2014.

3.3 An expert's report must be verified by a statement of truth in the following form –

I confirm that I have made clear which facts and matters referred to in this report are within my own knowledge and which are not. Those that are within my own knowledge I confirm to be true. The opinions I have expressed represent my true and complete professional opinions on the matters to which they refer.

Part 22 deals with statements of truth. Rule 32.14 sets out the consequences of verifying a document containing a false statement without an honest belief in its truth.)

Information

4 Under rule 35.9 the court may direct a party with access to information, which is not reasonably available to another party to serve on that other party a document, which records the information. The document served must include sufficient details of all the facts, tests, experiments and assumptions which underlie any part of the information to enable the party on whom it is served to make, or to obtain, a proper interpretation of the information and an assessment of its significance.

Instructions

5 Cross-examination of experts on the contents of their instructions will not be allowed unless the court permits it (or unless the party who gave the instructions consents). Before it gives permission the court must be satisfied that there are reasonable grounds to consider that the statement in the report of the substance of the instructions is inaccurate or incomplete. If the court is so satisfied, it will allow the cross-examination where it appears to be in the interests of justice.

Questions to Experts

6.1 Where a party sends a written question or questions under rule 35.6 direct to an expert, a copy of the questions must, at the same time, be sent to the other party or parties.

6.2 The party or parties instructing the expert must pay any fees charged by that expert for answering questions put under rule 35.6. This does not affect any decision of the court as to the party who is ultimately to bear the expert's fees.

Single joint expert

7 When considering whether to give permission for the parties to rely on expert evidence and whether that evidence should be from a single joint expert the court will take into account all the circumstances in particular, whether:

(a) it is proportionate to have separate experts for each party on a particular issue with reference to –

(i) the amount in dispute;

(ii) the importance to the parties; and

(iii) the complexity of the issue;

(b) the instruction of a single joint expert is likely to assist the parties and the court to resolve the issue more speedily and in a more cost-effective way than separately instructed experts;

(c) expert evidence is to be given on the issue of liability, causation or quantum;

(d) the expert evidence falls within a substantially established area of knowledge which is unlikely to be in dispute or there is likely to be a range of expert opinion;

(e) a party has already instructed an expert on the issue in question and whether or not that was done in compliance with any practice direction or relevant pre-action protocol;

(f) questions put in accordance with rule 35.6 are likely to remove the need for the other party to instruct an expert if one party has already instructed an expert;

(g) questions put to a single joint expert may not conclusively deal with all issues that may require testing prior to trial;

(h) a conference may be required with the legal representatives, experts and other witnesses which may make instruction of a single joint expert impractical; and

(i) a claim to privilege(GL) makes the instruction of any expert as a single joint expert inappropriate.

Orders

8 Where an order requires an act to be done by an expert, or otherwise affects an expert, the party instructing that expert must serve a copy of the order on the expert. The claimant must serve the order on a single joint expert.

Discussions between experts

9.1 Unless directed by the court discussions between experts are not mandatory. Parties must consider, with their experts, at an early stage, whether there is likely to be any useful purpose in holding an experts' discussion and if so when.

9.2 The purpose of discussions between experts is not for experts to settle cases but to agree and narrow issues and in particular to identify:

(i) the extent of the agreement between them;

(ii) the points of and short reasons for any disagreement;

(iii) action, if any, which may be taken to resolve any outstanding points of disagreement; and

(iv) any further material issues not raised and the extent to which these issues are agreed.

9.3 Where the experts are to meet, the parties must discuss and if possible agree whether an agenda is necessary, and if so attempt to agree one that helps the experts to focus on the issues which need to be discussed. The agenda must not be in the form of leading questions or hostile in tone.

9.4 Unless ordered by the court, or agreed by all parties, and the experts, neither the parties nor their legal representatives may attend experts discussions.

9.5 If the legal representatives do attend –

(i) they should not normally intervene in the discussion, except to answer questions put to them by the experts or to advise on the law; and

(ii) the experts may if they so wish hold part of their discussions in the absence of the legal representatives.

9.6 A statement must be prepared by the experts dealing with paragraphs 9.2(i) - (iv) above. Individual copies of the statements must be signed by the experts at the conclusion of the discussion, or as soon thereafter as practicable, and in any event within 7 days. Copies of the statements must be provided to the parties no later than 14 days after signing.

9.7 Experts must give their own opinions to assist the court and do not require the authority of the parties to sign a joint statement.

9.8 If an expert significantly alters an opinion, the joint statement must include a note or addendum by that expert explaining the change of opinion.

Assessors

10.1 An assessor may be appointed to assist the court under rule 35.15. Not less than 21 days before making any such appointment, the court will notify each party in writing of the name of the proposed assessor, of the matter in respect of which the assistance of the assessor will be sought and of the qualifications of the assessor to give that assistance.

10.2 Where any person has been proposed for appointment as an assessor, any party may object to that person either personally or in respect of that person's qualification.

10.3 Any such objection must be made in writing and filed with the court within 7 days of receipt of the notification referred to in paragraph 10.1 and will be taken into account by the court in deciding whether or not to make the appointment.

10.4 Copies of any report prepared by the assessor will be sent to each of the parties but the assessor will not give oral evidence or be open to cross-examination or questioning.

Concurrent expert evidence

11.1 At any stage in the proceedings the court may direct that some or all of the experts from like disciplines shall give their evidence concurrently. The following procedure shall then apply.

11.2 The court may direct that the parties agree an agenda for the taking of concurrent evidence, based upon the areas of disagreement identified in the experts' joint statements made pursuant to rule 35.12.

11.3 At the appropriate time the relevant experts will each take the oath or affirm. Unless the court orders otherwise, the experts will then address the items on the agenda in the manner set out in paragraph 11.4.

11.4 In relation to each issue on the agenda, and subject to the judge's discretion to modify the procedure –

(1) the judge may initiate the discussion by asking the experts, in turn, for their views. Once an expert has expressed a view the judge may ask questions about it. At one or more appropriate stages when questioning a particular expert, the judge may invite the other expert to comment or to ask that expert's own questions of the first expert;

(2) after the process set out in (1) has been completed for all the experts, the parties' representatives may ask questions of them. While such questioning may be designed to test the correctness of an expert's view, or seek clarification of it, it should not cover ground which has been fully explored already. In general a full cross-examination or re-examination is neither necessary nor appropriate; and

(3) after the process set out in (2) has been completed, the judge may summarise the experts' different positions on the issue and ask them to confirm or correct that summary.

Appendix 7: Record keeping checklists

Examination Checklist (Items in Bold are reserved for NEW PATIENT exam)

- Medical History (updated)
- Smoking history
- Alcohol consumption
- Caries risk status
- Happy with appearance

PDH

- **Can Patient Chew Ok?**
- **Have they had ortho?**
- **Ever had endo?**
- **Any implants?**
- **Any gum disease?**
- **OHI regime?**
- **Apprehensive?**

Reason for attending or C/o

E/O Exam

- Nodes
- E/o ST
- TMJ
- MOM

I/O Exam

- ST
- Teeth present + restorations
- Prosthesis?
- Caries?
- Mobility?
- Occlusal exam
- Tooth wear
- BPE/Perio chart
- FI
- BOP
- PI
- Caries Risk assessment

- Consent
- Treatment plan
- Treatment options (with risk benefits)
- Diet advice
- OHI
- Oral cancer prevention

<u>Where required</u>

- Radiographs
- Vitality tests
- CCS
- Symptomatic teeth
- Diagnosis
- Prognosis
- Notes signed

Endodontic Checklist

- Presenting symptoms,
- history of the present complaint with a dental history related to this,
- results of clinical examination and sensitivity tests,
- report on radiographs taken (see radiograph checklist),
- diagnosis
- treatment plan.
- Where there are alternative treatments or special problems, these should be explained and discussed with the patient along with the likely prognosis and recorded. It is good practice to provide the patient with written information. It should be recorded that the patient has agreed to the treatment and to the cost.
- Record of treatment
- use of local anaesthesia (see LA checklist),
- method of rubber dam isolation,
- notable findings (e.g. cracks or iatrogenic defects),
- working length of canals and their reference points,
- size to which canals are prepared,
- preparation technique,
- volume and concentration of irrigation used,
- dressing applied,
- type of temporary restoration,
- medication prescribed including analgesics and antibiotics (where indicated),
- root filling material,
- sealer and technique,
- number of radiographs,
- reports on radiographs taken,
- complications (e.g. iatrogenic incidents) and advice on final restoration or type of restoration (in case treatment is not performed by a specialist).
- Review
- The outcome of the treatment should be reviewed periodically and recorded

Local Anaesthetic Checklist

Warn of risks associated with numbness

LA used:

Type of injection:

Volume administered

Batch number and expiry date*

Radiographic checklist

Justification (what are you looking for)

Type of radiograph taken

What was found?

Any other abnormalities of note

Q&A score

*no actual legal requirement to record batch numbers in the notes, but recommended to keep a record somewhere (for example as part of stock control) - see **European Regulation 726/2004**

Periodontal Checklist

- Family History of periodontal disease
- Smoking/tobacco history
- Diet
- Regular attender?
- Other risk factors
- Reason for attending or C/o
- Consent
- Treatment plan
- Treatment options (with risk benefits)
- Diet advice
- OHI
- Classify and diagnose the periodontal disease

PDH – Can Patient Chew Ok?

– Any implants?
– OHI regime?

I/O Exam

- Gingival health
- Teeth present. Mark prognosis - Good(G), Uncertain(U), Hopeless(H)
- Prosthesis?
- Risk of root Caries?
- Mobility
- Occlusal exam
- Tooth wear
- BPE/Periodontal chart
- FI
- BOP
- PI
- Vitality tests

Radiographs (see checklist)

- Degree of bone loss: if the apex is visible then bone loss should be measured and reported as a
- percentage
- Pattern or type of bone loss: e.g. horizontal bone loss or angular (vertical) defects
- Presence of furcation defects
- Presence of

- Symptomatic teeth

Treatment

- Smoking cessation advice given
- OHI (specifics of what recommended)
- Record any photos taken
- Record warnings given
- LA administered (See LA checklist)
- Treatment done with length of appointment
- Antimicrobials advise

subgingival calculus

- Other features: e.g. perio-endo lesions; widened periodontal ligament spaces; abnormal root
- length or root morphology; overhanging restorations.

Appendix 8: Records Retention Periods

Area	Timescale	Law/guidance
Building and engineering works, inclusive of major projects abandoned or deferred - key records, (e.g. Final accounts, surveys, site plans, bills of quantities) + town and country planning matters and all formal contract documents	Permanent	The general principle to be followed in regard to these records is that they should be preserved for the life of the buildings and installations to which they refer.
Buildings - papers relating to occupation (but not Health 7 Safety information)	**3**	After occupation ceases. Construction Design Management Regulations 1994
Cash books	**6**	
Contracts - Non sealed (Property + other) on termination	**6**	The Limitation Act 1980
Contracts - sealed	Contracts under seal and associated records should be kept for a minimum of **15** years	These documents must be considered for permanent preservation but advice on appropriate place of deposit is to be obtained before any final decision is made
Debtors records – cleared	**2**	
Debtors records – uncleared	**6**	

Deeds of Title	Permanent	
Engineering works	Permanent	
Equipment	**11**	Consumer Protection Act 1987
Establishment records (personal files, contracts references & related correspondence)	**6**	After subject leaves service or until his/her 70th birthday – whichever is later
Establishment records (attendance, annual leave, timesheets etc.)	**2**	
Inspection Reports - e.g. Boilers, lifts etc.	Lifetime	Normally retain for the lifetime of an installation
Invoices	**6**	
Job Advertisements	**1**	
Job Applications (following termination of employment)	**3**	
Job descriptions (following termination of employment)	**3**	
Land Surveys/Registers	These documents must be considered for permanent preservation but advice on appropriate place of deposit is to be obtained before any final decision is made	
Litigation Dossiers (complaints including accident reports)	**10**	Where legal action has been commenced, keep as advised by legal representatives
Manuals	Lifetime	
Manuals - policy and procedure	Permanent	
Mortgage documents	Permanent	

(acquisition, transfer and disposal)		
Pay Roll	**6**	
Plans - Building	Permanent	
Receipts	**6**	
Receipt for registered and recorded delivery mail	**1.5**	
Software licenses	Lifetime	
Structure Plans	Permanent	
Tax forms	**6**	
VAT records	**6**	
Wages/Salary records	**10**	

Appendix 9: Child Protection flow chart

Child Protection and the Dental Team: Flowchart for action

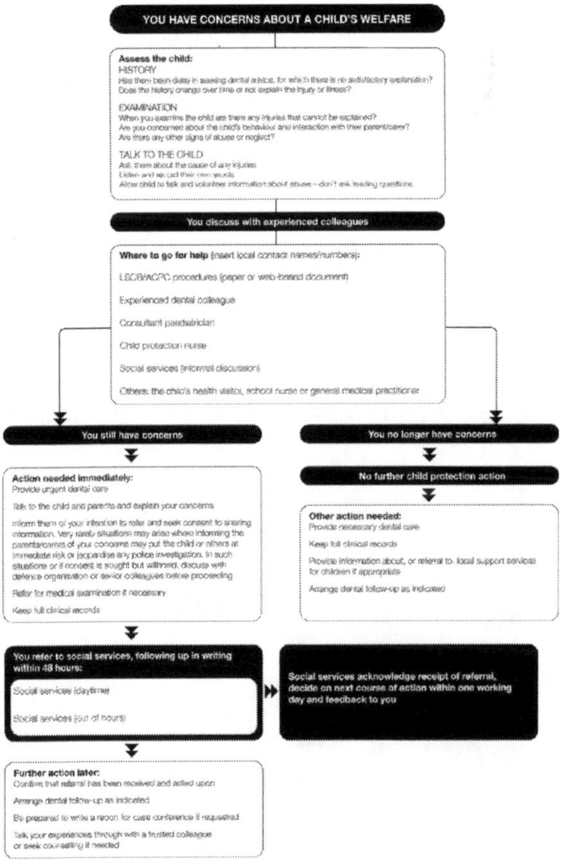

Appendix 10: Legislation that impacts the provision of dentistry

Autism Act 2009

The Care Act 2014

Care Quality Commission (Registration Requirements) Regulations 2009

The Care Quality Commission (Registration and Membership) (Amendment) Regulations 2012

Children Act 2004

Civil Contingences Act 2004

Companies Act 2006

Control of Substances hazardous to Health regulations 2002

The Controlled Drugs (Supervision of Management and Use) Regulations 2013

Data Protection Act 1998

Dentists Act 1984

The Electricity at Work regulations 1989

Employment Rights Act 1996

Equality Act 2010

Freedom of Information Act 2000 HSCA 17

The Gas Safety (Installation and Use) regulations 1998

The Hazardous Waste (England and Wales) Regulations 2005

The Health and Social Care Act 2008 (Regulated Activities) Regulations 2014

The Health and Social Care Act 2008 (Regulated Activities) (Amendment) Regulations

Health Professional Council – legal framework

Health and Safety at Work etc. Act 1974

The Health and Safety (First-Aid) Regulations 1981

The Health and Safety (Miscellaneous Amendments) 2002

Health and Social Work Professions Order 2001

Human Rights Act 1998

The Human Tissue Act 2004

The Human Tissue Authority codes of practice

The Ionising Radiations Regulations 1999

The Ionising Radiation (Medical Exposure) Regulations 2000

The Local Authority Social Services and National Health Service complaints (England) regulations 2009

Management of Health and Safety at Work Regulations 1999

The Manual Handling Operations Regulations 1992

The Health and Safety (Miscellaneous Amendments) 2002

Medical Act 1983

The Medical Devices Regulations 2002

The Medical Devices (Amendment) Regulations 2012

Medicines Act 1968

The Human Medicines Regulations 2012

Mental Capacity Act 2005

Mental Capacity Act Code of Practice

Mental Health Act 2007

Code of Practice (Mental Health Act 1983)

Misuse of Drugs Act 1971

The Misuse of Drugs and Misuse of Drugs (Safe Custody) (Amendment) Regulations 200

NHS Provider Licence May 2014

Public Interest Disclosure Act 1998

RIDDOR

Safeguarding Vulnerable Groups Act 2006

The Workplace (Health, Safety and Welfare) Regulations 1992

National health Service Act 1977

The Health and Safety (Miscellaneous Amendments) Regulations 2002

The National Health Service (General Dental Services Contracts) Regulations 2005

The National Health Service (Personal Dental Services Agreements) Regulations 2005

The National Health Service (General Dental Services Contracts) (Wales) Regulations 2006

The National Health Service (Personal Dental Services Agreements) (Wales) Regulations 2006

The National Health Service (Dental Charges) Regulations 2005

Appendix 11 - CQC Duty of Candour

This comes from Regulation 20 of the Health and Social Care Act 2008. Basically it states that every healthcare professional must be open and honest with their patients when something goes wrong with their treatment or when something has the potential to cause harm and distress.

The duty of candour requires notification by the registered person to the CQC when they become aware of (unintended or unexpected) events which could or which could appear to result in:

- **The death of a patient**
- **Severe or moderate harm to a patient** (root in sinus? Hypo accident?)
- **Prolonged psychological harm to a patient**

Failure to provide such notification is an offence and may lead to a fine of £2500

Appendix 12 - Did the GDC get it wrong?

The GDC are governed by the Dentist Act 1984, and whilst they are allowed to set standards, they are not allowed to contradict existing law. Let's have a look at a few examples:

1: In the Scope of practice document, the GDC state that "Dental nurses can apply fluoride varnish either on prescription from a dentist **or direct as part of a structured dental health program**". That last highlighted bit is perhaps something that needs to be addressed. Duraphat 50g/ml is a prescription only medicine. Under the Human Medicines Regulations 2012, dental nurses are not allowed to supply POM's direct to patients without a dentist's prescription, which potentially might occur in a structured dental health program. So one would need to check how that structured dental health program was run.

2: Can hygienist/therapists actually do anything under Direct Access? Well probably not, and some would see it as the GDC trying their best to meet the criticism in the 2012 Office of Fair Trading report that stated the arrangement for hygienists and therapists were "anti=competitive, restrictive and acting against the interest of consumers". They can't diagnose and they can't use local anaesthetic without a dentist's prescription (written instruction) due to the Medicines Act 1968. Direct access isn't even available under NHS contract. But but but what about "Patient Group Directions?"….yeah, good luck with that.

Appendix 13 - GDPR Checklist

- Conduct an information audit to map data flows
- Document what personal data you hold, where it comes from, who you share it with and what you do with it
- Identify the lawful basis by which you process and document personal data
- Review how you ask for and record consent
- Have a system to record and manage ongoing consent
- Make sure you are registered with ICO
- Provide privacy notices to individuals
- Have a process to recognise and respond to an individual's request to access their personal data
- Have a process to ensure that the personal data you hold remains accurate and up to date
- Have a system to securely dispose of personal data that is no longer required or where an individual has asked you to erase it
- Have a system in place to respond to an individual's request to restrict the processing of their personal data
- Have a system to allow individuals to move, copy or transfer their personal data from one IT environment to another in a safe and secure way, without hindrance to usability.
- Have a system to handle an individual's objection to the processing of their personal data
- Identify whether any of your processing operations constitute automated decision making and have systems in place to deal with the requirements.
- Have an appropriate data protection policy.
- Monitor your own compliance with data protection policies and regularly review the effectiveness of data handling and security controls

- Provides data protection awareness training for all staff
- Have a written contract with any data processors you use
- Manage information risks in a structured way so that management understands the business impact of personal data related risks and manages them effectively.
- Implement appropriate technical and organisational measures to integrate data protection into your processing activities
- Conduct a Data Protection Impact Assessment(DPIA) and have processes in place to action this
- Have a DPIA framework which links to your existing risk management and project management processes
- Nominate a data protection lead or Data Protection Officer (DPO)
- Have an information security policy supported by appropriate security measures
- Have an adequate level of protection for any personal data processed by others on your behalf that is transferred outside the European Economic Area
- Have effective processes to identify, report, manage and resolve any personal data breaches

Checking the principles

☐ We have identified an appropriate lawful basis (or bases) for our processing.

☐ If we are processing special category data or criminal offence data, we have identified a condition for processing this type of data.

☐ We don't do anything generally unlawful with personal data.

☐ We have considered how the processing may affect the individuals concerned and can justify any adverse impact.

☐ We only handle people's data in ways they would reasonably expect, or we can explain why any unexpected processing is justified.

☐ We do not deceive or mislead people when we collect their personal data.

☐ We are open and honest, and comply with the transparency obligations of the right to be informed.

☐ We have clearly identified our purpose or purposes for processing.

☐ We have documented those purposes.

☐ We include details of our purposes in our privacy information for individuals.

☐ We regularly review our processing and, where necessary, update our documentation and our privacy information for individuals.

☐ If we plan to use personal data for a new purpose, we check that this is compatible with our original purpose or we get specific consent for the new purpose.

☐ We only collect personal data we actually need for our specified purposes.

☐ We have sufficient personal data to properly fulfil those purposes.

☐ We periodically review the data we hold, and delete anything we don't need.

☐ We ensure the accuracy of any personal data we create.

☐ We have appropriate processes in place to check the accuracy of the data we collect, and we record the source of that data.

☐ We have a process in place to identify when we need to keep the data updated to properly fulfil our purpose, and we update it as necessary.

☐ If we need to keep a record of a mistake, we clearly identify it as a mistake.

☐ Our records clearly identify any matters of opinion, and where appropriate whose opinion it is and any relevant changes to the underlying facts.

☐ We comply with the individual's right to rectification and carefully consider any challenges to the accuracy of the personal data.

☐ As a matter of good practice, we keep a note of any challenges to the accuracy of the personal data.

☐ We know what personal data we hold and why we need it.

☐ We carefully consider and can justify how long we keep personal data.

☐ We have a policy with standard retention periods where possible, in line with documentation obligations.

☐ We regularly review our information and erase or anonymise personal data when we no longer need it.

☐ We have appropriate processes in place to comply with individuals' requests for erasure under 'the right to be forgotten'.

☐ We clearly identify any personal data that we need to keep for public interest archiving, scientific or historical research, or statistical purposes.

An online checklist can be found at - **https://ico.org.uk/for-organisations/resources-and-support/data-protection-self-assessment/**

If you have enjoyed this book, could I ask that you give me an Amazon review. It helps me know that this book has been of use and means I can get the feedback I need to write more books.

Thank you

MESSAGES FROM DENTAL MASTERS 2

Co-Authors Included in this book:

Glenys Bridges
Colin Campbell
Ian Dunn
Tony Gedge
Anoop Maini
Mark Oborn
Chris Orr
Susie Sanderson OBE
Prem-Pal Sehmi
Michael Young
Monik Vasant
And many more….

Compiled by :
Stephen Hudson
Foreword by:
Mark Topley

How To Enjoy And Thrive In Your Dental Career

40% of the net profits from the sale of this book will be given to the charity Bridge 2 Aid

bridge2aid

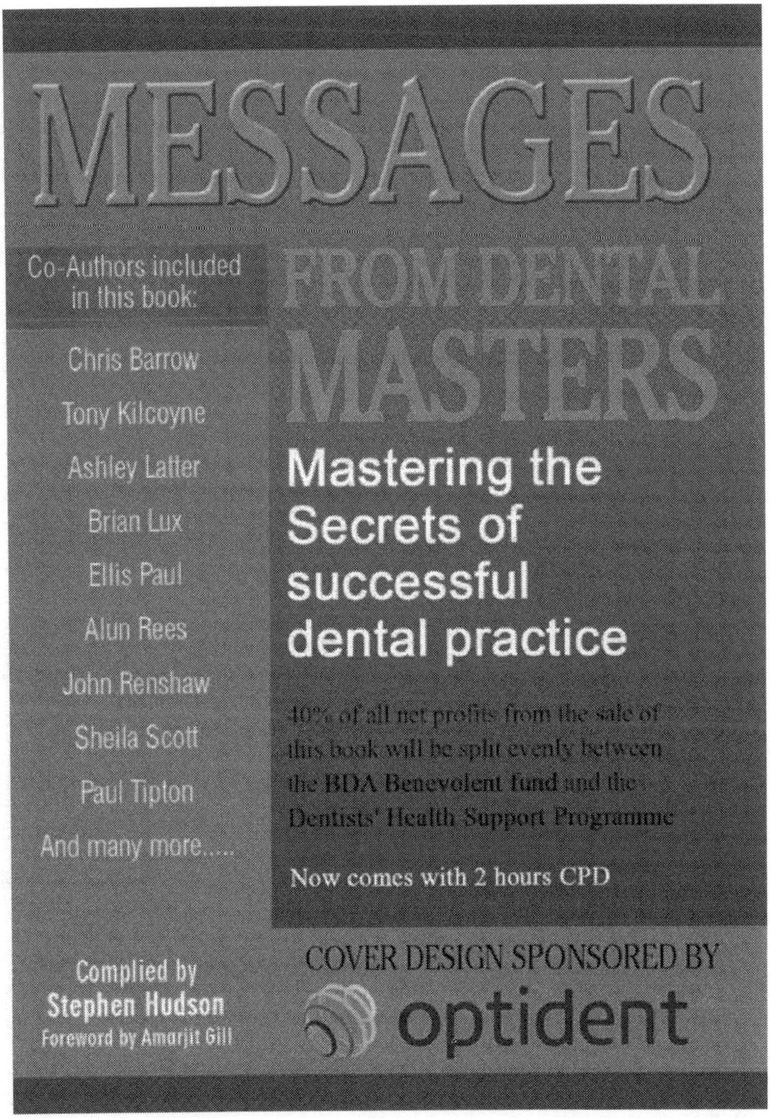
MESSAGES
FROM DENTAL
MASTERS
Co-Authors included in this book:
Chris Barrow
Tony Kilcoyne
Ashley Latter
Brian Lux
Ellis Paul
Alun Rees
John Renshaw
Sheila Scott
Paul Tipton
And many more.....
Mastering the Secrets of successful dental practice
40% of all net profits from the sale of this book will be split evenly between the BDA Benevolent fund and the Dentists' Health Support Programme
Now comes with 2 hours CPD
Complied by
Stephen Hudson
Foreword by Amarjit Gill
COVER DESIGN SPONSORED BY
optident

Printed in Dunstable, United Kingdom

91344188R00161